C-826 CAREER EXAMINATION SERIES

This is your
PASSBOOK for...

Typist

Test Preparation Study Guide
Questions & Answers

COPYRIGHT NOTICE

This book is SOLELY intended for, is sold ONLY to, and its use is RESTRICTED to individual, bona fide applicants or candidates who qualify by virtue of having seriously filed applications for appropriate license, certificate, professional and/or promotional advancement, higher school matriculation, scholarship, or other legitimate requirements of education and/or governmental authorities.

This book is NOT intended for use, class instruction, tutoring, training, duplication, copying, reprinting, excerption, or adaptation, etc., by:

1) Other publishers
2) Proprietors and/or Instructors of "Coaching" and/or Preparatory Courses
3) Personnel and/or Training Divisions of commercial, industrial, and governmental organizations
4) Schools, colleges, or universities and/or their departments and staffs, including teachers and other personnel
5) Testing Agencies or Bureaus
6) Study groups which seek by the purchase of a single volume to copy and/or duplicate and/or adapt this material for use by the group as a whole without having purchased individual volumes for each of the members of the group
7) Et al.

Such persons would be in violation of appropriate Federal and State statutes.

PROVISION OF LICENSING AGREEMENTS – Recognized educational, commercial, industrial, and governmental institutions and organizations, and others legitimately engaged in educational pursuits, including training, testing, and measurement activities, may address request for a licensing agreement to the copyright owners, who will determine whether, and under what conditions, including fees and charges, the materials in this book may be used them. In other words, a licensing facility exists for the legitimate use of the material in this book on other than an individual basis. However, it is asseverated and affirmed here that the material in this book CANNOT be used without the receipt of the express permission of such a licensing agreement from the Publishers. Inquiries re licensing should be addressed to the company, attention rights and permissions department.

All rights reserved, including the right of reproduction in whole or in part, in any form or by any means, electronic or mechanical, including photocopying, recording, or by any information storage and retrieval system, without permission in writing from the Publisher.

Copyright © 2025 by
National Learning Corporation

212 Michael Drive, Syosset, NY 11791
(516) 921-8888 • www.passbooks.com
E-mail: info@passbooks.com

PASSBOOK® SERIES

THE *PASSBOOK® SERIES* has been created to prepare applicants and candidates for the ultimate academic battlefield – the examination room.

At some time in our lives, each and every one of us may be required to take an examination – for validation, matriculation, admission, qualification, registration, certification, or licensure.

Based on the assumption that every applicant or candidate has met the basic formal educational standards, has taken the required number of courses, and read the necessary texts, the *PASSBOOK® SERIES* furnishes the one special preparation which may assure passing with confidence, instead of failing with insecurity. Examination questions – together with answers – are furnished as the basic vehicle for study so that the mysteries of the examination and its compounding difficulties may be eliminated or diminished by a sure method.

This book is meant to help you pass your examination provided that you qualify and are serious in your objective.

The entire field is reviewed through the huge store of content information which is succinctly presented through a provocative and challenging approach – the question-and-answer method.

A climate of success is established by furnishing the correct answers at the end of each test.

You soon learn to recognize types of questions, forms of questions, and patterns of questioning. You may even begin to anticipate expected outcomes.

You perceive that many questions are repeated or adapted so that you can gain acute insights, which may enable you to score many sure points.

You learn how to confront new questions, or types of questions, and to attack them confidently and work out the correct answers.

You note objectives and emphases, and recognize pitfalls and dangers, so that you may make positive educational adjustments.

Moreover, you are kept fully informed in relation to new concepts, methods, practices, and directions in the field.

You discover that you are actually taking the examination all the time: you are preparing for the examination by "taking" an examination, not by reading extraneous and/or supererogatory textbooks.

In short, this PASSBOOK®, used directedly, should be an important factor in helping you to pass your test.

TYPIST

DUTIES AND RESPONSIBILITIES
Under direct supervision, with little latitude for independent or unreviewed action or decision, performs typing work and related clerical duties of ordinary difficulty and responsibility; performs related work.

EXAMPLES OF WORK:
Receives and organizes work to be typed determining document format; types correspondence, documents, records, and other written material in final or draft form using handwritten, rough drafts, marked copy, oral recordings, or data from various equipment as the source material; proofreads and corrects work producing accurate, clean, and complete typed copy; prepares, stores, and retrieves lists and documents; answers telephone and gives out routine information or relieves at switchboard;

SUBJECT OF EXAMINATION
Written test will cover knowledge, skills and/or abilities in such areas as:
1. Spelling;
2. English grammar and usage; punctuation;
3. Office record keeping;
4. Clerical abilities;
5. Alphabetizing;
6. Keyboarding practices; and
7. Using good judgment in the provision of office support services.

HOW TO TAKE A TEST

I. YOU MUST PASS AN EXAMINATION

A. WHAT EVERY CANDIDATE SHOULD KNOW

Examination applicants often ask us for help in preparing for the written test. What can I study in advance? What kinds of questions will be asked? How will the test be given? How will the papers be graded?

As an applicant for a civil service examination, you may be wondering about some of these things. Our purpose here is to suggest effective methods of advance study and to describe civil service examinations.

Your chances for success on this examination can be increased if you know how to prepare. Those "pre-examination jitters" can be reduced if you know what to expect. You can even experience an adventure in good citizenship if you know why civil service exams are given.

B. WHY ARE CIVIL SERVICE EXAMINATIONS GIVEN?

Civil service examinations are important to you in two ways. As a citizen, you want public jobs filled by employees who know how to do their work. As a job seeker, you want a fair chance to compete for that job on an equal footing with other candidates. The best-known means of accomplishing this two-fold goal is the competitive examination.

Exams are widely publicized throughout the nation. They may be administered for jobs in federal, state, city, municipal, town or village governments or agencies.

Any citizen may apply, with some limitations, such as the age or residence of applicants. Your experience and education may be reviewed to see whether you meet the requirements for the particular examination. When these requirements exist, they are reasonable and applied consistently to all applicants. Thus, a competitive examination may cause you some uneasiness now, but it is your privilege and safeguard.

C. HOW ARE CIVIL SERVICE EXAMS DEVELOPED?

Examinations are carefully written by trained technicians who are specialists in the field known as "psychological measurement," in consultation with recognized authorities in the field of work that the test will cover. These experts recommend the subject matter areas or skills to be tested; only those knowledges or skills important to your success on the job are included. The most reliable books and source materials available are used as references. Together, the experts and technicians judge the difficulty level of the questions.

Test technicians know how to phrase questions so that the problem is clearly stated. Their ethics do not permit "trick" or "catch" questions. Questions may have been tried out on sample groups, or subjected to statistical analysis, to determine their usefulness.

Written tests are often used in combination with performance tests, ratings of training and experience, and oral interviews. All of these measures combine to form the best-known means of finding the right person for the right job.

II. HOW TO PASS THE WRITTEN TEST

A. NATURE OF THE EXAMINATION

To prepare intelligently for civil service examinations, you should know how they differ from school examinations you have taken. In school you were assigned certain definite pages to read or subjects to cover. The examination questions were quite detailed and usually emphasized memory. Civil service exams, on the other hand, try to discover your present ability to perform the duties of a position, plus your potentiality to learn these duties. In other words, a civil service exam attempts to predict how successful you will be. Questions cover such a broad area that they cannot be as minute and detailed as school exam questions.

In the public service similar kinds of work, or positions, are grouped together in one "class." This process is known as *position-classification*. All the positions in a class are paid according to the salary range for that class. One class title covers all of these positions, and they are all tested by the same examination.

B. FOUR BASIC STEPS

1) Study the announcement

How, then, can you know what subjects to study? Our best answer is: "Learn as much as possible about the class of positions for which you've applied." The exam will test the knowledge, skills and abilities needed to do the work.

Your most valuable source of information about the position you want is the official exam announcement. This announcement lists the training and experience qualifications. Check these standards and apply only if you come reasonably close to meeting them.

The brief description of the position in the examination announcement offers some clues to the subjects which will be tested. Think about the job itself. Review the duties in your mind. Can you perform them, or are there some in which you are rusty? Fill in the blank spots in your preparation.

Many jurisdictions preview the written test in the exam announcement by including a section called "Knowledge and Abilities Required," "Scope of the Examination," or some similar heading. Here you will find out specifically what fields will be tested.

2) Review your own background

Once you learn in general what the position is all about, and what you need to know to do the work, ask yourself which subjects you already know fairly well and which need improvement. You may wonder whether to concentrate on improving your strong areas or on building some background in your fields of weakness. When the announcement has specified "some knowledge" or "considerable knowledge," or has used adjectives like "beginning principles of…" or "advanced … methods," you can get a clue as to the number and difficulty of questions to be asked in any given field. More questions, and hence broader coverage, would be included for those subjects which are more important in the work. Now weigh your strengths and weaknesses against the job requirements and prepare accordingly.

3) Determine the level of the position

Another way to tell how intensively you should prepare is to understand the level of the job for which you are applying. Is it the entering level? In other words, is this the position in which beginners in a field of work are hired? Or is it an intermediate or advanced level? Sometimes this is indicated by such words as "Junior" or "Senior" in the class title. Other jurisdictions use Roman numerals to designate the level – Clerk I, Clerk II, for example. The word "Supervisor" sometimes appears in the title. If the level is not indicated by the title, check the description of duties. Will you be working under very close supervision, or will you have responsibility for independent decisions in this work?

4) Choose appropriate study materials

Now that you know the subjects to be examined and the relative amount of each subject to be covered, you can choose suitable study materials. For beginning level jobs, or even advanced ones, if you have a pronounced weakness in some aspect of your training, read a modern, standard textbook in that field. Be sure it is up to date and has general coverage. Such books are normally available at your library, and the librarian will be glad to help you locate one. For entry-level positions, questions of appropriate difficulty are chosen – neither highly advanced questions, nor those too simple. Such questions require careful thought but not advanced training.

If the position for which you are applying is technical or advanced, you will read more advanced, specialized material. If you are already familiar with the basic principles of your field, elementary textbooks would waste your time. Concentrate on advanced textbooks and technical periodicals. Think through the concepts and review difficult problems in your field.

These are all general sources. You can get more ideas on your own initiative, following these leads. For example, training manuals and publications of the government agency which employs workers in your field can be useful, particularly for technical and professional positions. A letter or visit to the government department involved may result in more specific study suggestions, and certainly will provide you with a more definite idea of the exact nature of the position you are seeking.

III. KINDS OF TESTS

Tests are used for purposes other than measuring knowledge and ability to perform specified duties. For some positions, it is equally important to test ability to make adjustments to new situations or to profit from training. In others, basic mental abilities not dependent on information are essential. Questions which test these things may not appear as pertinent to the duties of the position as those which test for knowledge and information. Yet they are often highly important parts of a fair examination. For very general questions, it is almost impossible to help you direct your study efforts. What we can do is to point out some of the more common of these general abilities needed in public service positions and describe some typical questions.

1) General information

Broad, general information has been found useful for predicting job success in some kinds of work. This is tested in a variety of ways, from vocabulary lists to questions about current events. Basic background in some field of work, such as sociology or economics, may be sampled in a group of questions. Often these are principles which have become familiar to most persons through exposure rather than through formal training. It is difficult to advise you how to study for these questions; being alert to the world around you is our best suggestion.

2) Verbal ability

An example of an ability needed in many positions is verbal or language ability. Verbal ability is, in brief, the ability to use and understand words. Vocabulary and grammar tests are typical measures of this ability. Reading comprehension or paragraph interpretation questions are common in many kinds of civil service tests. You are given a paragraph of written material and asked to find its central meaning.

3) Numerical ability

Number skills can be tested by the familiar arithmetic problem, by checking paired lists of numbers to see which are alike and which are different, or by interpreting charts and graphs. In the latter test, a graph may be printed in the test booklet which you are asked to use as the basis for answering questions.

4) Observation

A popular test for law-enforcement positions is the observation test. A picture is shown to you for several minutes, then taken away. Questions about the picture test your ability to observe both details and larger elements.

5) Following directions

In many positions in the public service, the employee must be able to carry out written instructions dependably and accurately. You may be given a chart with several columns, each column listing a variety of information. The questions require you to carry out directions involving the information given in the chart.

6) Skills and aptitudes

Performance tests effectively measure some manual skills and aptitudes. When the skill is one in which you are trained, such as typing or shorthand, you can practice. These tests are often very much like those given in business school or high school courses. For many of the other skills and aptitudes, however, no short-time preparation can be made. Skills and abilities natural to you or that you have developed throughout your lifetime are being tested.

Many of the general questions just described provide all the data needed to answer the questions and ask you to use your reasoning ability to find the answers. Your best preparation for these tests, as well as for tests of facts and ideas, is to be at your physical and mental best. You, no doubt, have your own methods of getting into an exam-taking mood and keeping "in shape." The next section lists some ideas on this subject.

IV. KINDS OF QUESTIONS

Only rarely is the "essay" question, which you answer in narrative form, used in civil service tests. Civil service tests are usually of the short-answer type. Full instructions for answering these questions will be given to you at the examination. But in case this is your first experience with short-answer questions and separate answer sheets, here is what you need to know:

1) Multiple-choice Questions

Most popular of the short-answer questions is the "multiple choice" or "best answer" question. It can be used, for example, to test for factual knowledge, ability to solve problems or judgment in meeting situations found at work.

A multiple-choice question is normally one of three types—

- It can begin with an incomplete statement followed by several possible endings. You are to find the one ending which *best* completes the statement, although some of the others may not be entirely wrong.
- It can also be a complete statement in the form of a question which is answered by choosing one of the statements listed.

- It can be in the form of a problem – again you select the best answer.

Here is an example of a multiple-choice question with a discussion which should give you some clues as to the method for choosing the right answer:

When an employee has a complaint about his assignment, the action which will *best* help him overcome his difficulty is to
- A. discuss his difficulty with his coworkers
- B. take the problem to the head of the organization
- C. take the problem to the person who gave him the assignment
- D. say nothing to anyone about his complaint

In answering this question, you should study each of the choices to find which is best. Consider choice "A" – Certainly an employee may discuss his complaint with fellow employees, but no change or improvement can result, and the complaint remains unresolved. Choice "B" is a poor choice since the head of the organization probably does not know what assignment you have been given, and taking your problem to him is known as "going over the head" of the supervisor. The supervisor, or person who made the assignment, is the person who can clarify it or correct any injustice. Choice "C" is, therefore, correct. To say nothing, as in choice "D," is unwise. Supervisors have and interest in knowing the problems employees are facing, and the employee is seeking a solution to his problem.

2) True/False Questions

The "true/false" or "right/wrong" form of question is sometimes used. Here a complete statement is given. Your job is to decide whether the statement is right or wrong.

SAMPLE: A roaming cell-phone call to a nearby city costs less than a non-roaming call to a distant city.

This statement is wrong, or false, since roaming calls are more expensive.

This is not a complete list of all possible question forms, although most of the others are variations of these common types. You will always get complete directions for answering questions. Be sure you understand *how* to mark your answers – ask questions until you do.

V. RECORDING YOUR ANSWERS

Computer terminals are used more and more today for many different kinds of exams.

For an examination with very few applicants, you may be told to record your answers in the test booklet itself. Separate answer sheets are much more common. If this separate answer sheet is to be scored by machine – and this is often the case – it is highly important that you mark your answers correctly in order to get credit.

An electronic scoring machine is often used in civil service offices because of the speed with which papers can be scored. Machine-scored answer sheets must be marked with a pencil, which will be given to you. This pencil has a high graphite content which responds to the electronic scoring machine. As a matter of fact, stray dots may register as answers, so do not let your pencil rest on the answer sheet while you are pondering the correct answer. Also, if your pencil lead breaks or is otherwise defective, ask for another.

Since the answer sheet will be dropped in a slot in the scoring machine, be careful not to bend the corners or get the paper crumpled.

The answer sheet normally has five vertical columns of numbers, with 30 numbers to a column. These numbers correspond to the question numbers in your test booklet. After each number, going across the page are four or five pairs of dotted lines. These short dotted lines have small letters or numbers above them. The first two pairs may also have a "T" or "F" above the letters. This indicates that the first two pairs only are to be used if the questions are of the true-false type. If the questions are multiple choice, disregard the "T" and "F" and pay attention only to the small letters or numbers.

Answer your questions in the manner of the sample that follows:

32. The largest city in the United States is
   A. Washington, D.C.
   B. New York City
   C. Chicago
   D. Detroit
   E. San Francisco

1) Choose the answer you think is best. (New York City is the largest, so "B" is correct.)
2) Find the row of dotted lines numbered the same as the question you are answering. (Find row number 32)
3) Find the pair of dotted lines corresponding to the answer. (Find the pair of lines under the mark "B.")
4) Make a solid black mark between the dotted lines.

VI. BEFORE THE TEST

Common sense will help you find procedures to follow to get ready for an examination. Too many of us, however, overlook these sensible measures. Indeed, nervousness and fatigue have been found to be the most serious reasons why applicants fail to do their best on civil service tests. Here is a list of reminders:

- Begin your preparation early – Don't wait until the last minute to go scurrying around for books and materials or to find out what the position is all about.
- Prepare continuously – An hour a night for a week is better than an all-night cram session. This has been definitely established. What is more, a night a week for a month will return better dividends than crowding your study into a shorter period of time.
- Locate the place of the exam – You have been sent a notice telling you when and where to report for the examination. If the location is in a different town or otherwise unfamiliar to you, it would be well to inquire the best route and learn something about the building.
- Relax the night before the test – Allow your mind to rest. Do not study at all that night. Plan some mild recreation or diversion; then go to bed early and get a good night's sleep.
- Get up early enough to make a leisurely trip to the place for the test – This way unforeseen events, traffic snarls, unfamiliar buildings, etc. will not upset you.
- Dress comfortably – A written test is not a fashion show. You will be known by number and not by name, so wear something comfortable.

- Leave excess paraphernalia at home – Shopping bags and odd bundles will get in your way. You need bring only the items mentioned in the official notice you received; usually everything you need is provided. Do not bring reference books to the exam. They will only confuse those last minutes and be taken away from you when in the test room.
- Arrive somewhat ahead of time – If because of transportation schedules you must get there very early, bring a newspaper or magazine to take your mind off yourself while waiting.
- Locate the examination room – When you have found the proper room, you will be directed to the seat or part of the room where you will sit. Sometimes you are given a sheet of instructions to read while you are waiting. Do not fill out any forms until you are told to do so; just read them and be prepared.
- Relax and prepare to listen to the instructions
- If you have any physical problem that may keep you from doing your best, be sure to tell the test administrator. If you are sick or in poor health, you really cannot do your best on the exam. You can come back and take the test some other time.

VII. AT THE TEST

The day of the test is here and you have the test booklet in your hand. The temptation to get going is very strong. Caution! There is more to success than knowing the right answers. You must know how to identify your papers and understand variations in the type of short-answer question used in this particular examination. Follow these suggestions for maximum results from your efforts:

1) Cooperate with the monitor

The test administrator has a duty to create a situation in which you can be as much at ease as possible. He will give instructions, tell you when to begin, check to see that you are marking your answer sheet correctly, and so on. He is not there to guard you, although he will see that your competitors do not take unfair advantage. He wants to help you do your best.

2) Listen to all instructions

Don't jump the gun! Wait until you understand all directions. In most civil service tests you get more time than you need to answer the questions. So don't be in a hurry. Read each word of instructions until you clearly understand the meaning. Study the examples, listen to all announcements and follow directions. Ask questions if you do not understand what to do.

3) Identify your papers

Civil service exams are usually identified by number only. You will be assigned a number; you must not put your name on your test papers. Be sure to copy your number correctly. Since more than one exam may be given, copy your exact examination title.

4) Plan your time

Unless you are told that a test is a "speed" or "rate of work" test, speed itself is usually not important. Time enough to answer all the questions will be provided, but this does not mean that you have all day. An overall time limit has been set. Divide the total time (in minutes) by the number of questions to determine the approximate time you have for each question.

5) Do not linger over difficult questions

If you come across a difficult question, mark it with a paper clip (useful to have along) and come back to it when you have been through the booklet. One caution if you do this – be sure to skip a number on your answer sheet as well. Check often to be sure that you have not lost your place and that you are marking in the row numbered the same as the question you are answering.

6) Read the questions

Be sure you know what the question asks! Many capable people are unsuccessful because they failed to *read* the questions correctly.

7) Answer all questions

Unless you have been instructed that a penalty will be deducted for incorrect answers, it is better to guess than to omit a question.

8) Speed tests

It is often better NOT to guess on speed tests. It has been found that on timed tests people are tempted to spend the last few seconds before time is called in marking answers at random – without even reading them – in the hope of picking up a few extra points. To discourage this practice, the instructions may warn you that your score will be "corrected" for guessing. That is, a penalty will be applied. The incorrect answers will be deducted from the correct ones, or some other penalty formula will be used.

9) Review your answers

If you finish before time is called, go back to the questions you guessed or omitted to give them further thought. Review other answers if you have time.

10) Return your test materials

If you are ready to leave before others have finished or time is called, take ALL your materials to the monitor and leave quietly. Never take any test material with you. The monitor can discover whose papers are not complete, and taking a test booklet may be grounds for disqualification.

VIII. EXAMINATION TECHNIQUES

1) Read the general instructions carefully. These are usually printed on the first page of the exam booklet. As a rule, these instructions refer to the timing of the examination; the fact that you should not start work until the signal and must stop work at a signal, etc. If there are any *special* instructions, such as a choice of questions to be answered, make sure that you note this instruction carefully.

2) When you are ready to start work on the examination, that is as soon as the signal has been given, read the instructions to each question booklet, underline any key words or phrases, such as *least, best, outline, describe* and the like. In this way you will tend to answer as requested rather than discover on reviewing your paper that you *listed without describing*, that you selected the *worst* choice rather than the *best* choice, etc.

3) If the examination is of the objective or multiple-choice type – that is, each question will also give a series of possible answers: A, B, C or D, and you are called upon to select the best answer and write the letter next to that answer on your answer paper – it is advisable to start answering each question in turn. There may be anywhere from 50 to 100 such questions in the three or four hours allotted and you can see how much time would be taken if you read through all the questions before beginning to answer any. Furthermore, if you come across a question or group of questions which you know would be difficult to answer, it would undoubtedly affect your handling of all the other questions.

4) If the examination is of the essay type and contains but a few questions, it is a moot point as to whether you should read all the questions before starting to answer any one. Of course, if you are given a choice – say five out of seven and the like – then it is essential to read all the questions so you can eliminate the two that are most difficult. If, however, you are asked to answer all the questions, there may be danger in trying to answer the easiest one first because you may find that you will spend too much time on it. The best technique is to answer the first question, then proceed to the second, etc.

5) Time your answers. Before the exam begins, write down the time it started, then add the time allowed for the examination and write down the time it must be completed, then divide the time available somewhat as follows:
   - If 3-1/2 hours are allowed, that would be 210 minutes. If you have 80 objective-type questions, that would be an average of 2-1/2 minutes per question. Allow yourself no more than 2 minutes per question, or a total of 160 minutes, which will permit about 50 minutes to review.
   - If for the time allotment of 210 minutes there are 7 essay questions to answer, that would average about 30 minutes a question. Give yourself only 25 minutes per question so that you have about 35 minutes to review.

6) The most important instruction is to *read each question* and make sure you know what is wanted. The second most important instruction is to *time yourself properly* so that you answer every question. The third most important instruction is to *answer every question*. Guess if you have to but include something for each question. Remember that you will receive no credit for a blank and will probably receive some credit if you write something in answer to an essay question. If you guess a letter – say "B" for a multiple-choice question – you may have guessed right. If you leave a blank as an answer to a multiple-choice question, the examiners may respect your feelings but it will not add a point to your score. Some exams may penalize you for wrong answers, so in such cases *only*, you may not want to guess unless you have some basis for your answer.

7) Suggestions
   a. Objective-type questions
      1. Examine the question booklet for proper sequence of pages and questions
      2. Read all instructions carefully
      3. Skip any question which seems too difficult; return to it after all other questions have been answered
      4. Apportion your time properly; do not spend too much time on any single question or group of questions

5. Note and underline key words – *all, most, fewest, least, best, worst, same, opposite,* etc.
6. Pay particular attention to negatives
7. Note unusual option, e.g., unduly long, short, complex, different or similar in content to the body of the question
8. Observe the use of "hedging" words – *probably, may, most likely,* etc.
9. Make sure that your answer is put next to the same number as the question
10. Do not second-guess unless you have good reason to believe the second answer is definitely more correct
11. Cross out original answer if you decide another answer is more accurate; do not erase until you are ready to hand your paper in
12. Answer all questions; guess unless instructed otherwise
13. Leave time for review

  b. Essay questions
    1. Read each question carefully
    2. Determine exactly what is wanted. Underline key words or phrases.
    3. Decide on outline or paragraph answer
    4. Include many different points and elements unless asked to develop any one or two points or elements
    5. Show impartiality by giving pros and cons unless directed to select one side only
    6. Make and write down any assumptions you find necessary to answer the questions
    7. Watch your English, grammar, punctuation and choice of words
    8. Time your answers; don't crowd material

8) Answering the essay question

Most essay questions can be answered by framing the specific response around several key words or ideas. Here are a few such key words or ideas:

M's: manpower, materials, methods, money, management
P's: purpose, program, policy, plan, procedure, practice, problems, pitfalls, personnel, public relations

  a. Six basic steps in handling problems:
    1. Preliminary plan and background development
    2. Collect information, data and facts
    3. Analyze and interpret information, data and facts
    4. Analyze and develop solutions as well as make recommendations
    5. Prepare report and sell recommendations
    6. Install recommendations and follow up effectiveness

  b. Pitfalls to avoid
    1. *Taking things for granted* – A statement of the situation does not necessarily imply that each of the elements is necessarily true; for example, a complaint may be invalid and biased so that all that can be taken for granted is that a complaint has been registered

2. *Considering only one side of a situation* – Wherever possible, indicate several alternatives and then point out the reasons you selected the best one
3. *Failing to indicate follow up* – Whenever your answer indicates action on your part, make certain that you will take proper follow-up action to see how successful your recommendations, procedures or actions turn out to be
4. *Taking too long in answering any single question* – Remember to time your answers properly

IX. AFTER THE TEST

Scoring procedures differ in detail among civil service jurisdictions although the general principles are the same. Whether the papers are hand-scored or graded by machine we have described, they are nearly always graded by number. That is, the person who marks the paper knows only the number – never the name – of the applicant. Not until all the papers have been graded will they be matched with names. If other tests, such as training and experience or oral interview ratings have been given, scores will be combined. Different parts of the examination usually have different weights. For example, the written test might count 60 percent of the final grade, and a rating of training and experience 40 percent. In many jurisdictions, veterans will have a certain number of points added to their grades.

After the final grade has been determined, the names are placed in grade order and an eligible list is established. There are various methods for resolving ties between those who get the same final grade – probably the most common is to place first the name of the person whose application was received first. Job offers are made from the eligible list in the order the names appear on it. You will be notified of your grade and your rank as soon as all these computations have been made. This will be done as rapidly as possible.

People who are found to meet the requirements in the announcement are called "eligibles." Their names are put on a list of eligible candidates. An eligible's chances of getting a job depend on how high he stands on this list and how fast agencies are filling jobs from the list.

When a job is to be filled from a list of eligibles, the agency asks for the names of people on the list of eligibles for that job. When the civil service commission receives this request, it sends to the agency the names of the three people highest on this list. Or, if the job to be filled has specialized requirements, the office sends the agency the names of the top three persons who meet these requirements from the general list.

The appointing officer makes a choice from among the three people whose names were sent to him. If the selected person accepts the appointment, the names of the others are put back on the list to be considered for future openings.

That is the rule in hiring from all kinds of eligible lists, whether they are for typist, carpenter, chemist, or something else. For every vacancy, the appointing officer has his choice of any one of the top three eligibles on the list. This explains why the person whose name is on top of the list sometimes does not get an appointment when some of the persons lower on the list do. If the appointing officer chooses the second or third eligible, the No. 1 eligible does not get a job at once, but stays on the list until he is appointed or the list is terminated.

X. HOW TO PASS THE INTERVIEW TEST

The examination for which you applied requires an oral interview test. You have already taken the written test and you are now being called for the interview test – the final part of the formal examination.

You may think that it is not possible to prepare for an interview test and that there are no procedures to follow during an interview. Our purpose is to point out some things you can do in advance that will help you and some good rules to follow and pitfalls to avoid while you are being interviewed.

What is an interview supposed to test?

The written examination is designed to test the technical knowledge and competence of the candidate; the oral is designed to evaluate intangible qualities, not readily measured otherwise, and to establish a list showing the relative fitness of each candidate – as measured against his competitors – for the position sought. Scoring is not on the basis of "right" and "wrong," but on a sliding scale of values ranging from "not passable" to "outstanding." As a matter of fact, it is possible to achieve a relatively low score without a single "incorrect" answer because of evident weakness in the qualities being measured.

Occasionally, an examination may consist entirely of an oral test – either an individual or a group oral. In such cases, information is sought concerning the technical knowledges and abilities of the candidate, since there has been no written examination for this purpose. More commonly, however, an oral test is used to supplement a written examination.

Who conducts interviews?

The composition of oral boards varies among different jurisdictions. In nearly all, a representative of the personnel department serves as chairman. One of the members of the board may be a representative of the department in which the candidate would work. In some cases, "outside experts" are used, and, frequently, a businessman or some other representative of the general public is asked to serve. Labor and management or other special groups may be represented. The aim is to secure the services of experts in the appropriate field.

However the board is composed, it is a good idea (and not at all improper or unethical) to ascertain in advance of the interview who the members are and what groups they represent. When you are introduced to them, you will have some idea of their backgrounds and interests, and at least you will not stutter and stammer over their names.

What should be done before the interview?

While knowledge about the board members is useful and takes some of the surprise element out of the interview, there is other preparation which is more substantive. It *is* possible to prepare for an oral interview – in several ways:

1) Keep a copy of your application and review it carefully before the interview

This may be the only document before the oral board, and the starting point of the interview. Know what education and experience you have listed there, and the sequence and dates of all of it. Sometimes the board will ask you to review the highlights of your experience for them; you should not have to hem and haw doing it.

2) Study the class specification and the examination announcement

Usually, the oral board has one or both of these to guide them. The qualities, characteristics or knowledges required by the position sought are stated in these documents. They offer valuable clues as to the nature of the oral interview. For example, if the job involves supervisory responsibilities, the announcement will usually indicate that knowledge of modern supervisory methods and the qualifications of the candidate as a supervisor will be tested. If so, you can expect such questions, frequently in the form of a hypothetical situation which you are expected to solve. NEVER go into an oral without knowledge of the duties and responsibilities of the job you seek.

3) Think through each qualification required

Try to visualize the kind of questions you would ask if you were a board member. How well could you answer them? Try especially to appraise your own knowledge and background in each area, *measured against the job sought*, and identify any areas in which you are weak. Be critical and realistic – do not flatter yourself.

4) Do some general reading in areas in which you feel you may be weak

For example, if the job involves supervision and your past experience has NOT, some general reading in supervisory methods and practices, particularly in the field of human relations, might be useful. Do NOT study agency procedures or detailed manuals. The oral board will be testing your understanding and capacity, not your memory.

5) Get a good night's sleep and watch your general health and mental attitude

You will want a clear head at the interview. Take care of a cold or any other minor ailment, and of course, no hangovers.

What should be done on the day of the interview?

Now comes the day of the interview itself. Give yourself plenty of time to get there. Plan to arrive somewhat ahead of the scheduled time, particularly if your appointment is in the fore part of the day. If a previous candidate fails to appear, the board might be ready for you a bit early. By early afternoon an oral board is almost invariably behind schedule if there are many candidates, and you may have to wait. Take along a book or magazine to read, or your application to review, but leave any extraneous material in the waiting room when you go in for your interview. In any event, relax and compose yourself.

The matter of dress is important. The board is forming impressions about you – from your experience, your manners, your attitude, and your appearance. Give your personal appearance careful attention. Dress your best, but not your flashiest. Choose conservative, appropriate clothing, and be sure it is immaculate. This is a business interview, and your appearance should indicate that you regard it as such. Besides, being well groomed and properly dressed will help boost your confidence.

Sooner or later, someone will call your name and escort you into the interview room. *This is it.* From here on you are on your own. It is too late for any more preparation. But remember, you asked for this opportunity to prove your fitness, and you are here because your request was granted.

What happens when you go in?

The usual sequence of events will be as follows: The clerk (who is often the board stenographer) will introduce you to the chairman of the oral board, who will introduce you to the other members of the board. Acknowledge the introductions before you sit down. Do not be surprised if you find a microphone facing you or a stenotypist sitting by. Oral interviews are usually recorded in the event of an appeal or other review.

Usually the chairman of the board will open the interview by reviewing the highlights of your education and work experience from your application – primarily for the benefit of the other members of the board, as well as to get the material into the record. Do not interrupt or comment unless there is an error or significant misinterpretation; if that is the case, do not hesitate. But do not quibble about insignificant matters. Also, he will usually ask you some question about your education, experience or your present job – partly to get you to start talking and to establish the interviewing "rapport." He may start the actual questioning, or turn it over to one of the other members. Frequently, each member undertakes the questioning on a particular area, one in which he is perhaps most competent, so you can expect each member to participate in the examination. Because time is limited, you may also expect some rather abrupt switches in the direction the questioning takes, so do not be upset by it. Normally, a board member will not pursue a single line of questioning unless he discovers a particular strength or weakness.

After each member has participated, the chairman will usually ask whether any member has any further questions, then will ask you if you have anything you wish to add. Unless you are expecting this question, it may floor you. Worse, it may start you off on an extended, extemporaneous speech. The board is not usually seeking more information. The question is principally to offer you a last opportunity to present further qualifications or to indicate that you have nothing to add. So, if you feel that a significant qualification or characteristic has been overlooked, it is proper to point it out in a sentence or so. Do not compliment the board on the thoroughness of their examination – they have been sketchy, and you know it. If you wish, merely say, "No thank you, I have nothing further to add." This is a point where you can "talk yourself out" of a good impression or fail to present an important bit of information. Remember, *you close the interview yourself.*

The chairman will then say, "That is all, Mr. _____, thank you." Do not be startled; the interview is over, and quicker than you think. Thank him, gather your belongings and take your leave. Save your sigh of relief for the other side of the door.

How to put your best foot forward
Throughout this entire process, you may feel that the board individually and collectively is trying to pierce your defenses, seek out your hidden weaknesses and embarrass and confuse you. Actually, this is not true. They are obliged to make an appraisal of your qualifications for the job you are seeking, and they want to see you in your best light. Remember, they must interview all candidates and a non-cooperative candidate may become a failure in spite of their best efforts to bring out his qualifications. Here are 15 suggestions that will help you:

1) Be natural – Keep your attitude confident, not cocky
If you are not confident that you can do the job, do not expect the board to be. Do not apologize for your weaknesses, try to bring out your strong points. The board is interested in a positive, not negative, presentation. Cockiness will antagonize any board member and make him wonder if you are covering up a weakness by a false show of strength.

2) Get comfortable, but don't lounge or sprawl
Sit erectly but not stiffly. A careless posture may lead the board to conclude that you are careless in other things, or at least that you are not impressed by the importance of the occasion. Either conclusion is natural, even if incorrect. Do not fuss with your clothing, a pencil or an ashtray. Your hands may occasionally be useful to emphasize a point; do not let them become a point of distraction.

3) Do not wisecrack or make small talk
This is a serious situation, and your attitude should show that you consider it as such. Further, the time of the board is limited – they do not want to waste it, and neither should you.

4) Do not exaggerate your experience or abilities

In the first place, from information in the application or other interviews and sources, the board may know more about you than you think. Secondly, you probably will not get away with it. An experienced board is rather adept at spotting such a situation, so do not take the chance.

5) If you know a board member, do not make a point of it, yet do not hide it

Certainly you are not fooling him, and probably not the other members of the board. Do not try to take advantage of your acquaintanceship – it will probably do you little good.

6) Do not dominate the interview

Let the board do that. They will give you the clues – do not assume that you have to do all the talking. Realize that the board has a number of questions to ask you, and do not try to take up all the interview time by showing off your extensive knowledge of the answer to the first one.

7) Be attentive

You only have 20 minutes or so, and you should keep your attention at its sharpest throughout. When a member is addressing a problem or question to you, give him your undivided attention. Address your reply principally to him, but do not exclude the other board members.

8) Do not interrupt

A board member may be stating a problem for you to analyze. He will ask you a question when the time comes. Let him state the problem, and wait for the question.

9) Make sure you understand the question

Do not try to answer until you are sure what the question is. If it is not clear, restate it in your own words or ask the board member to clarify it for you. However, do not haggle about minor elements.

10) Reply promptly but not hastily

A common entry on oral board rating sheets is "candidate responded readily," or "candidate hesitated in replies." Respond as promptly and quickly as you can, but do not jump to a hasty, ill-considered answer.

11) Do not be peremptory in your answers

A brief answer is proper – but do not fire your answer back. That is a losing game from your point of view. The board member can probably ask questions much faster than you can answer them.

12) Do not try to create the answer you think the board member wants

He is interested in what kind of mind you have and how it works – not in playing games. Furthermore, he can usually spot this practice and will actually grade you down on it.

13) Do not switch sides in your reply merely to agree with a board member

Frequently, a member will take a contrary position merely to draw you out and to see if you are willing and able to defend your point of view. Do not start a debate, yet do not surrender a good position. If a position is worth taking, it is worth defending.

14) Do not be afraid to admit an error in judgment if you are shown to be wrong

The board knows that you are forced to reply without any opportunity for careful consideration. Your answer may be demonstrably wrong. If so, admit it and get on with the interview.

15) Do not dwell at length on your present job

The opening question may relate to your present assignment. Answer the question but do not go into an extended discussion. You are being examined for a *new* job, not your present one. As a matter of fact, try to phrase ALL your answers in terms of the job for which you are being examined.

Basis of Rating

Probably you will forget most of these "do's" and "don'ts" when you walk into the oral interview room. Even remembering them all will not ensure you a passing grade. Perhaps you did not have the qualifications in the first place. But remembering them will help you to put your best foot forward, without treading on the toes of the board members.

Rumor and popular opinion to the contrary notwithstanding, an oral board wants you to make the best appearance possible. They know you are under pressure – but they also want to see how you respond to it as a guide to what your reaction would be under the pressures of the job you seek. They will be influenced by the degree of poise you display, the personal traits you show and the manner in which you respond.

ABOUT THIS BOOK

This book contains tests divided into Examination Sections. Go through each test, answering every question in the margin. We have also attached a sample answer sheet at the back of the book that can be removed and used. At the end of each test look at the answer key and check your answers. On the ones you got wrong, look at the right answer choice and learn. Do not fill in the answers first. Do not memorize the questions and answers, but understand the answer and principles involved. On your test, the questions will likely be different from the samples. Questions are changed and new ones added. If you understand these past questions you should have success with any changes that arise. Tests may consist of several types of questions. We have additional books on each subject should more study be advisable or necessary for you. Finally, the more you study, the better prepared you will be. This book is intended to be the last thing you study before you walk into the examination room. Prior study of relevant texts is also recommended. NLC publishes some of these in our Fundamental Series. Knowledge and good sense are important factors in passing your exam. Good luck also helps. So now study this Passbook, absorb the material contained within and take that knowledge into the examination. Then do your best to pass that exam.

EXAMINATION SECTION

EXAMINATION SECTION

TEST 1

DIRECTIONS: Each question or incomplete statement is followed by several suggested answers or completions. Select the one that BEST answers the question or completes the statement. *PRINT THE LETTER OF THE CORRECT ANSWER IN THE SPACE AT THE RIGHT.*

1. The ∧ or caret symbol is a proofreader's mark which means that a
    A. space should have been left between two words
    B. new paragraph should be indicated
    C. word, phrase, or punctuation mark should be inserted
    D. word that is abbreviated should be spelled out

2. Of the following items, the one which should NOT be omitted from a typed inter-office memorandum is the
    A. salutation
    B. complementary closing
    C. formal signature
    D. names of those to receive copies

3. A typed rough draft should be double-spaced and should have wide margins PRIMARILY in order to
    A. save time in making typing corrections
    B. provide room for making insertions and corrections
    C. insure that the report is well-organized
    D. permit faster typing of the draft

4. In tabular reports, when a main heading, secondary heading, and single line of columnar headings are used, a triple space (2 blank lines) would be used after the _____ heading(s).
    A. main
    B. secondary
    C. columnar
    D. main and secondary

5. You have been requested to type a letter to Mr. Brown, a district attorney of a small town.
    Of the following, the CORRECT salutation to use is Dear
    A. District Attorney Brown:
    B. Mr. District Attorney:
    C. Mr. Brown:
    D. Honorable Brown:

6. A form letter that is sent to the public can be made to look more personal in appearance by doing all of the following EXCEPT
    A. using a meter stamp on the envelope of the letter
    B. having the letter signed with pen and ink
    C. using a good quality of paper for the letter
    D. matching the type used in the letter with that used for fill-ins

7. A senior typist opens a word-processing application to instruct a typist to create a table that contains three column headings. Under each column heading are three items.
Of the following, which sequence should the senior typist tell the typist to use when creating this table?
    A. First type the headings, and then type the items under them, a column at a time
    B. type each heading with its column of items under it, one column at a time
    C. first type the column of items, then center the headings above them
    D. type the headings and items across the page line by line

8. When a letter is addressed to an agency and a particular person should see it, an *attention line* is used.
This attention line is USUALLY found
    A. on the envelope only
    B. above the address
    C. below the address
    D. after the agency named in the address

9. The typing technique of *justifying* is used to
    A. decide how wide margins of different sized letters should be
    B. make all the lines of copy end evenly on the right-hand margin
    C. center headings above columns on tabular typed material
    D. condense the amount of space that is needed to make a manuscript look presentable

10. The date line on a letter is typed correctly when the date is ALL on one line
    A. with the month written out
    B. with slashes between the numbers
    C. and the month is abbreviated
    D. with a period at the end

11. When considering how wide to make a column when typing a table, the BASIC rule to follow is that the column should be as wide as the longest
    A. item in the body of the column
    B. heading of all of the columns
    C. item in the body or heading of that column
    D. heading or the longest item in the body of any column on that page

12. When a lengthy quotation is included in a letter or a report, it must be indicated that it is quoted material. This may be done by
    A. enclosing the quotation in parentheses
    B. placing an exclamation point at the end of the quotation
    C. using the apostrophe marks
    D. indenting from the regular margins on the left and right

13. In order to reach the highest rate of speed and the greatest degree of accuracy while typing, it is LEAST important to
    A. maintain good posture
    B. keep the hands and arms at a comfortable level
    C. strike the keys evenly
    D. keep the typing action in the wrists

    13._____

14. It has been shown that the rate of typing and dictation drops when the secretary is not familiar with the language or topic of the copy.
    A practice that a supervisor might BEST advise to improve the knowledge and therefore increase the rate of typing dictation for such material would be for the secretary to
    A. plan a conference with her supervisor to discuss the subject matter
    B. read and review correspondence and related technical journals that come into the office
    C. recopy or retype previously transcribed material as practice
    D. withdraw sample materials from the files to take home for study

    14._____

15. The one of the following in which the tab key is NOT generally used is the
    A. placement of the complimentary close and signature line
    B. indentation of paragraphs
    C. placement of the date line
    D. centering of title headings

    15._____

16. In order for a business letter to be effective, it is LEAST important that it
    A. say what is meant simply and directly
    B. be written in formal language
    C. include all information the receiver needs to know
    D. be courteously written

    16._____

17. If you are momentarily called away from your desk while typing a report of a confidential nature, you should cover or turn the copy over and
    A. remove the page being typed from the computer and file the report
    B. ask someone to watch your desk for you
    C. close the document so that the page is not visible
    D. spread a folder over the computer screen to conceal it

    17._____

18. When typing a table that contains a column of figures and a column of words, the PROPER alignment of the column of figures and the column of words should be an even _____ the column of words.
    A. right-hand edge for the column of numbers and an even left-hand edge for
    B. right-hand edge for both the column of numbers and
    C. left-hand edge for the column of numbers and an even right-hand edge for
    D. left-hand edge for both the column of numbers and

    18._____

19. The word *re*, when used in a memorandum, refers to the information that is on the _____ line. 19.____
    A. identification   B. subject   C. attention   D. reference

20. Of the following uses of the period, the one which requires NO spacing after it when it is typed is when the period 20.____
    A. follows an abbreviation or an initial
    B. follows a figure or letter at the beginning of a line in a list of items
    C. comes between the initials that make up a single abbreviation
    D. comes at the end of a sentence

21. This mark is a proofreader's mark meaning the word 21.____
    A. is misspelled   B. should be underlined
    C. should be bold   D. should be capitalized

22. When typing a report that is double-spaced, the STANDARD recommended practice for indicating the start of new paragraphs is to 22.____
    A. double-space between paragraphs and indent the first word at least five spaces
    B. triple-space between paragraphs and indent the first word at least five spaces
    C. triple-space between paragraphs and type block style at the margin
    D. double-space between paragraphs and type block style at the margin

23. In order to center a heading on a sheet of paper once the center of the paper has been found, the EASIEST and MOST efficient method to use is 23.____
    A. note the scale at each end of the heading to be centered and divide by two
    B. backspace from the center of the paper one space for every two letters and spaces in the heading
    C. arrange the heading around the middle number on the computer
    D. use a ruler to mark off the amount of space from both sides of the center of the paper that should be taken up by the heading

24. You are about to type a single-spaced letter from a typewritten draft. In order to center this letter from top to bottom, your FIRST step should be to 24.____
    A. determine the number of spaces needed for the top and bottom margins
    B. determine the number of spaces needed for the left and right margins
    C. count the number of lines, including blank ones, which will be used for the letter
    D. subtract from the number of writing lines on the sheet of paper the number of lines that will not be used for the letter

25. When typing a table which lists several amounts of money and the total in a column, the dollar sign should be placed in front of the 25.____
    A. first dollar amount only
    B. total dollar amount only
    C. first and total dollar amounts only
    D. all of the amounts of money in the column

26. If a legal document is being prepared and requires necessary information to be typed into blank areas on preprinted legal forms, the margins for a line of typewritten material should be determined PRIMARILY by
    A. counting the total number of words to be typed
    B. the margins set for the pre-printed matter
    C. spacing backwards from the right margin rule
    D. the estimated width and height of the material to be entered

26.____

27. When checking for errors in material you've typed, it is BEST to
    A. proofread the material and use the spell-check function in combination
    B. give the material to someone else to review
    C. run the spell-check function and auto-correct all found errors
    D. proofread the material then e-mail it to another typist for final approval

27.____

28. Assume that Mr. Frank Foran is an acting official. In a letter written to him, the word *acting* would
    A. be used with the title in the address and in the salutation
    B. not be used with the title in the address
    C. be used with the title in the address but not in the salutation
    D. not be used with the title in the address or in the salutation

28.____

29. The software program that requires proficiency in typing in order to best utilize its MOST important features is
    A. Microsoft Excel   B. Adobe Reader
    C. Microsoft Word   D. Intuit QuickBooks

29.____

30. The MAIN reason for keeping a careful record of incoming mail is that
    A. greater speed and accuracy is obtained for answering outgoing mail
    B. this record is legal evidence
    C. it develops the efficiency of the office clerks
    D. the information may be useful some day

30.____

KEY (CORRECT ANSWERS)

1.	C	11.	C	21.	D
2.	D	12.	D	22.	A
3.	B	13.	D	23.	B
4.	B	14.	B	24.	C
5.	C	15.	D	25.	C
6.	A	16.	B	26.	B
7.	D	17.	C	27.	A
8.	C	18.	A	28.	C
9.	B	19.	B	29.	C
10.	A	20.	C	30.	A

TEST 2

DIRECTIONS: Each question or incomplete statement is followed by several suggested answers or completions. Select the one that BEST answers the question or completes the statement. *PRINT THE LETTER OF THE CORRECT ANSWER IN THE SPACE AT THE RIGHT.*

Questions 1-4.

DIRECTIONS: Questions 1 through 4 are to be answered SOLELY on the basis of the information contained in the following passage which is taken from a typing test.

Modern office methods, geared to ever higher speeds and aimed at ever greater efficiency, are largely the result of the typewriter. The typewriter is a substitute for handwriting; and, in the hands of a skilled typist, not only turns out letters and other documents at least three times faster than a penman can do the work, but turns out the greater volume more uniformly and legibly. With the use of carbon paper and onionskin paper, identical copies can be made at the same time.

The typewriter, besides its effect on the conduct of business and government, has had a very important effect on the position of women. The typewriter has done much to bring women into business and government, and today there are vastly more women than men typists. Many women have used the keys of the typewriter to climb the ladder to responsible managerial positions.

The typewriter, as its name implies, employs type to make an ink impression on paper. For many years, the manual typewriter was the standard machine used. Today, the electric typewriter is dominant, with electronic typewriters, word processors, and computers coming into wider use.

The mechanism of the office manual typewriter includes a set of keys arranged systematically in rows; a semicircular frame of type, connected to the keys by levers; the carriage or paper carrier; a rubber roller called a platen, against which the type strikes; and an inked ribbon which makes the impression of the type character when the key strikes it. This machine, once omnipresent, is an antique today.

1. The above passage mentions a number of good features of the combination of a skilled typist and a typewriter.
   Of the following, the feature which is NOT mentioned in the passage is
   A. speed   B. uniformity   C. reliability   D. legibility

   1.____

2. According to the above passage, a skilled typist can
   A. turn out at least five carbon copies of typed matter
   B. type at least three times faster than a penman can write
   C. type more than 80 words a minute
   D. readily move into a managerial position

   2.____

3. According to the above passage, which of the following is NOT part of the mechanism of a manual typewriter? 3.____
   A. Carbon paper
   B. Paper carrier
   C. Platen
   D. Inked ribbon

4. According to the above passage, the typewriter has helped 4.____
   A. men more than women in business
   B. women in career advancement into management
   C. men and women equally, but women have taken better advantage of it
   D. more women than men, because men generally dislike routine typing work

5. Standard rules for typing spacing have developed through usage. According to these rules, two spaces are left after a(n) 5.____
   A. colon
   B. comma
   C. hyphen
   D. opening parenthesis

6. Assume that you have to type the heading CENTERING TYPED HEADINGS on a piece of paper which extends from 0 to 100 on the typewriter scale. You want the heading to be perfectly centered on the paper. 6.____
   In order to find the proper point on the typewriter scale at which to begin typing, you should determine the paper's center point on the typewriter scale and then _____ the number of letters and spaces in the heading.
   A. add
   B. add one-half
   C. subtract
   D. subtract one-half

7. While typing from a rough draft, the practice of reading a line ahead of what you are now typing is considered to be a 7.____
   A. *good* practice; it may prepare your fingers for the words which you will be typing
   B. *good* practice; it may help you to review the subject matter contained in the material
   C. *poor* practice; it may increase your typing speed so that your accuracy is decreased
   D. *poor* practice; it may cause you to lose your concentration and make errors in the words you are presently typing

8. Assume that you are transcribing a letter and you are not sure how to divide a word at the end of a line you are typing. 8.____
   The BEST way to determine where to divide the word is by
   A. asking your supervisor
   B. asking the person who dictated the letter
   C. checking with other stenographers
   D. looking up the word in a dictionary

9. When taking proper care of a typewriter, it is NOT a desirable action to 9.____
   A. clean the feed rolls with a cloth
   B. dust the exterior surface of the machine
   C. oil the rubber parts of the machine
   D. use a type-cleaning brush to clean the keys

10. Of the following, the LEAST desirable action to take when typing a rough 10.____
    draft of a report is to
    A. cross out typing errors instead of erasing them
    B. double or triple space between lines
    C. provide large margins on all sides of the typing paper
    D. use letterhead or onionskin paper

11. The date line of every business letter should indicate the month, the day of 11.____
    the month, and the year.
    The MOST common practice when typing a date line is to type it as
    A. Jan. 12, 2018   B. January 12, 2018
    C. 1-12-18   D. 1/12/18

Questions 12-16.

DIRECTIONS: Questions 12 through 16 are to be answered SOLELY on the basis of the information provided in the following passage.

A written report is a communication of information from one person to another. It is an account of some matter especially investigated, however routine that matter may be. The ultimate basis of any good written report is facts, which became known through observation and verification. Good written reports may seem to be no more than general ideas and opinions. However, in such cases, the facts leading to these opinions were gathered, verified, and reported earlier, and the opinions are dependent upon these facts. Good style, proper form, and emphasis cannot make a good written report out of unreliable information and bad judgments but on the other hand, solid investigation and brilliant thinking are not likely to become very useful until they are effectively communicated to others. If a person's work calls for written reports, then his work is often no better than his written reports.

12. Based on the information in the above passage, it can be concluded that 12.____
    opinions expressed in a report should be
    A. based on facts which are gathered and reported
    B. emphasized repeatedly when they result from a special investigation
    C. kept to a minimum
    D. separated from the body of the report

13. In the above passage, the one of the following which is mentioned as a way 13.____
    of establishing facts is
    A. authority   B. communication
    C. reporting   D. verification

14. According to the above passage, the characteristic shared by ALL written reports is that they are
    A. accounts of routine matters
    B. transmissions of information
    C. reliable and logical
    D. written in proper form

14.____

15. Which of the following conclusions can LOGICALLY be drawn from the information given in the above passage?
    A. Brilliant thinking can make up for unreliable information in a report.
    B. One method of judging an individual's work is the quality of the written reports he is required to submit.
    C. Proper form and emphasis can make a good report out of unreliable information.
    D. Good written reports that seem to be no more than general ideas should be rewritten.

15.____

16. Which of the following suggested titles would be MOST appropriate for this passage?
    A. GATHERING AND ORGANIZING FACTS
    B. TECHNIQUES OF OBSERVATION
    C. NATURE AND PURPOSE OF REPORTS
    D. REPORTS AND OPINIONS: DIFFERENCES AND SIMILARITIES

16.____

Questions 17-25

DIRECTIONS: Each of Questions 17 through 25 consists of a sentence which may or may not be an example of good English usage. Examine each sentence, considering grammar, punctuation, spelling, capitalization, and awkwardness. Then choose the correct statement about it from the four choices below it. If the English usage in the sentence given is better than any of the changes suggested in Choices B, C, or D, pick choice A. Do NOT pick a choice that will change the meaning of the sentence.

17. We attended a staff conference on Wednesday the new safety and fire rules were discussed.
    A. This is an example of acceptable writing.
    B. The words *safety*, *fire*, and *rules* should begin with capital letters.
    C. There should be a comma after the word *Wednesday*.
    D. There should be a period after the word *Wednesday*, and the word *the* should begin with a capital letter.

17.____

18. Neither the dictionary or the telephone directory could be found in the office library.
    A. This is an example of acceptable writing.
    B. The word *or* should be changed to *nor*.
    C. The word *library* should be spelled *libery*.
    D. The word *neither* should be changed to *either*.

18.____

19. The report would have been typed correctly if the typist cold read the draft.
    A. This is an example of acceptable writing.
    B. The word *would* should be removed.
    C. The word *have* should be inserted after the word *could*.
    D. The word *correctly* should be changed to *correct*.

20. The supervisor brought the reports and forms to an employees desk.
    A. This is an example of acceptable writing.
    B. The word *brought* should be changed to *took*.
    C. There should be a comma after the word *reports* and a comma after the word *forms*.
    D. The word *employees* should be spelled *employee's*.

21. It's important for all the office personnel to submit their vacation schedules on time.
    A. This is an example of acceptable writing.
    B. The word *It's* should be spelled *Its*.
    C. The word *their* should be spelled *they're*.
    D. The word *personnel* should be spelled *personal*.

22. The supervisor wants that all staff members report to the office at 9:00 A.M.
    A. This is an example of acceptable writing.
    B. The word *that* should be removed and the word *to* should be inserted after the word *members*.
    C. There should be a comma after the word *wants* and a comma after the word *office*.
    D. The word *wants* should be changed to *want* and the word *shall* should be inserted after the word *members*.

23. Every morning the clerk opens the office mail and distributes it.
    A. This is an example of acceptable writing.
    B. The word *opens* should be changed to *open*.
    C. The word *mail* should be changed to *letters*.
    D. The word *it* should be changed to *them*.

24. The secretary typed more fast on an electric typewriter than on a manual typewriter.
    A. This is an example of acceptable writing.
    B. The words *more fast* should be changed to *faster*.
    C. There should be a comma after the words *electric typewriter*.
    D. The word *than* should be changed to *then*.

25. The new stenographer needed a desk a typewriter, a chair and a blotter.
    A. This is an example of acceptable writing.
    B. The word *blotter* should be spelled *blodder*.
    C. The word *stenographer* should begin with a capital letter.
    D. There should be a comma after the word *desk*.

KEY (CORRECT ANSWERS)

1. C
2. B
3. A
4. B
5. A

6. D
7. D
8. D
9. C
10. D

11. B
12. A
13. D
14. B
15. B

16. C
17. D
18. B
19. C
20. D

21. A
22. B
23. A
24. B
25. D

EXAMINATION SECTION
TEST 1

DIRECTIONS: Each question or incomplete statement is followed by several suggested answers or completions. Select the one that BEST answers the question or completes the statement. *PRINT THE LETTER OF THE CORRECT ANSWER IN THE SPACE AT THE RIGHT.*

Questions 1-10.

WORD MEANING

DIRECTIONS: Each question from 1 to 10 contains a word in capitals followed by four suggested meanings of the word. For each question, choose the best meaning. *PRINT THE LETTER OF THE CORRECT ANSWER IN THE SPACE AT THE RIGHT.*

1. ACCURATE
    A. correct   B. useful   C. afraid   D. careless

2. ALTER
    A. copy   B. change   C. report   D. agree

3. DOCUMENT
    A. outline   B. agreement   C. blueprint   D. record

4. INDICATE
    A. listen   B. show   C. guess   D. try

5. INVENTORY
    A. custom   B. discovery   C. warning   D. list

6. ISSUE
    A. annoy   B. use up   C. give out   D. gain

7. NOTIFY
    A. inform   B. promise   C. approve   D. strengthen

8. ROUTINE
    A. path   B. mistake   C. habit   D. journey

9. TERMINATE
    A. rest   B. start   C. deny   D. end

10. TRANSMIT
    A. put in   B. send   C. stop   D. go across

Questions 11-15.

READING COMPREHENSION

DIRECTIONS: Questions 11 through 15 test how well you understand what you read. It will be necessary for you to read carefully because your answers to these questions should be based ONLY on the information given in the following paragraphs.

The recipient gains an impression of a typewritten letter before he begins to read the message. Pastors which provide for a good first impression include margins and spacing that are visually pleasing, formal parts of the letter which are correctly placed according to the style of the letter, copy which is free of obvious erasures and over-strikes, and transcript that is even and clear. The problem for the typist is that of how to produce that first, positive impression of her work.

There are several general rules which a typist can follow when she wishes to prepare a properly spaced letter on a sheet of letter-head. Ordinarily, the width of a letter should not be less than four inches nor more than six inches. The side margins should also have a desirable relation to the bottom margin and the space between the letterhead and the body of the letter. Usually the most appealing arrangement is when the side margins are even and the bottom margin is slightly wider than the side margins. In some offices, however, standard line length is used for all business letters, and the secretary then varies the spacing between the date line and the inside address according to the length of the letter.

11. The BEST title for the above paragraphs would be:

    A. Writing Office Letters
    B. Making Good First Impressions
    C. Judging Well-Typed Letters
    D. Good Placing and Spacing for Office Letters

12. According to the above paragraphs, which of the following might be considered the way in which people very quickly judge the quality of work which has been typed? By

    A. measuring the margins to see if they are correct
    B. looking at the spacing and cleanliness of the typescript
    C. scanning the body of the letter for meaning
    D. reading the date line and address for errors

13. What, according to the above paragraphs, would be definitely UNDESIRABLE as the average line length of a typed letter?

    A. 4"   B. 5"   C. 6"   D. 7"

14. According to the above paragraphs, when the line length is kept standard, the secretary

    A. does not have to vary the spacing at all since this also is standard
    B. adjusts the spacing between the date line and inside address for different lengths of letters
    C. uses the longest line as a guideline for spacing between the date line and inside address
    D. varies the number of spaces between the lines

15. According to the above paragraphs, side margins are MOST pleasing when they
    A. are even and somewhat smaller than the bottom margin
    B. are slightly wider than the bottom margin
    C. vary with the length of the letter
    D. are figured independently from the letterhead and the body of the letter

Questions 16-20.

CODING

DIRECTIONS:

Name of Applicant	H A N G S B R U K E
Test Code	c o m p l e x i t y
File Number	0 1 2 3 4 5 6 7 8 9

Assume that each of the above capital letters is the first letter of the name of an Applicant, that the small letter directly beneath each capital letter is the test code for the Applicant, and that the number directly beneath each code letter is the file number for the Applicant.

In each of the following Questions 16 through 20, the test code letters and the file numbers in Columns 2 and 3 should correspond to the capital letters in Column 1. For each question, look at each column carefully and mark your answer as follows:

If there is an error only in Column 2, mark your answer A.
If there is an error only in Column 3, mark your answer B.
If there is an error in both Columns 2 and 3, mark your answer C.
If both Columns 2 and 3 are correct, mark your answer D.

The following sample question is given to help you understand the procedure.

SAMPLE QUESTION

Column 1	Column 2	Column 3
AKEHN	otyci	18902

In Column 2, the final test code letter *i.* should be m. Column 3 is correctly coded to Column 1. Since there is an error only in Column 2, the answer is A.

	Column 1	Column 2	Column 3
16.	NEKKU	mytti	29987
17.	KRAEB	txyle	86095
18.	ENAUK	ymoit	92178
19.	REANA	xeomo	69121
20.	EKHSE	ytcxy	97049

Questions 21-30.

ARITHMETICAL REASONING

21. If a secretary answered 28 phone calls and typed the addresses for 112 credit statements in one morning, what is the ratio of phone calls answered to credit statements typed for that period of time?

    A. 1:4   B. 1:7   C. 2:3   D. 3:5

22. According to a suggested filing system, no more than 10 folders should be filed behind any one file guide and from 15 to 25 file guides should be used in each file drawer for easy finding and filing.
    The maximum number of folders that a five-drawer file cabinet can hold to allow easy finding and filing is

    A. 550   B. 750   C. 1,100   D. 1,250

23. An employee had a starting salary of $25,804. He received a salary increase at the end of each year, and at the end of the seventh year his salary was $33,476.
    What was his average annual increase in salary over these seven years?

    A. $1,020   B. $1,076   C. $1,096   D. $1,144

24. The 55 typists and 28 senior clerks in a certain city agency were paid a total of $1,943,200 in salaries last year.
    If the average annual salary of a typist was $22,400 the average annual salary of a senior clerk was

    A. $25,400   B. $26,600   C. $26,800   D. $27,000

25. A typist has been given a three page report to type. She has finished typing the first two pages. The first page has 283 words, and the second page has 366 words.
    If the total report consists of 954 words, how many words will she have to type on the third page of the report?

    A. 202   B. 287   C. 305   D. 313

26. In one day, Clerk A processed 30% more forms than Clerk 8, and Clerk C processed 1 1/4 times as many forms as Clerk A. If Clerk B processed 40 forms, how many more forms were processed by Clerk C than Clerk B?

    A. 12   B. 13   C. 21   D. 25

27. A clerk who earns a gross salary of $452 every two weeks has the following deductions taken from her paycheck:
    15% for City, State, Federal taxes; 2 1/2% for Social Security; $1.30 for health insurance; and $6.00 for union dues. The amount of her take-home pay is

    A. $256.20   B. $312.40   C. $331.60   D. $365.60

28. In 2020, a city agency spent $2,000 to buy pencils at a cost of $5.00 a dozen.
    If the agency used 3/4 of these pencils in 2020 and used the same number of pencils in 2021, how many more pencils did it have to buy to have enough pencils for all of 2021?

    A. 1,200   B. 2,400   C. 3,600   D. 4,800

29. A clerk who worked in Agency X earned the following salaries: $20,140 the first year, $21,000 the second year, and $21,920 the third year. Another clerk who worked in Agency Y for three years earned $21,100 a year for two years and $21,448 the third year. The difference between the average salaries received by both clerks over a three-year period is

A. $196   B. $204   C. $348   D. $564

30. An employee who works over 40 hours in any week receives overtime payment for the extra hours at time and one-half (1 1/2 times) his hourly rate of pay. An employee who earns $13.60 an hour works a total of 45 hours during a certain week.
His total pay for that week would be

A. $564.40   B. $612.00   C. $646.00   D. $812.00

Questions 31-35.

RELATED INFORMATION

31. To tell a newly-employed clerk to fill a top drawer of a four-drawer cabinet with heavy folders which will be often used and to keep lower drawers only partly filled is

    A. *good,* because a tall person would have to bend unnecessarily if he had to use a lower drawer
    B. *bad,* because the file cabinet may tip over when the top drawer is opened
    C. *good,* because it is the most easily reachable drawer for the average person
    D. *bad,* because a person bending down at another drawer may accidentally bang his head on the bottom of the drawer when he straightens up

32. If a senior typist or senior clerk has requisitioned a *ream* of paper in order to duplicate a single page office announcement, how many announcements can be printed from the one package of paper?

    A. 200   B. 500   C. 700   0. 1,000

33. Your supervisor has asked you to locate a telephone number for an attorney named Jones, whose office is located at 311 Broadway, and whose name is not already listed in your files.
The BEST method for finding the number would be for you to

    A. call the information operator and have her get it for you
    B. look in the alphabetical directory (white pages) under the name Jones at 311 Broadway
    C. refer to the heading Attorney in the yellow pages for the name Jones at 311 Broadway
    D. ask your supervisor who referred her to Mr. Jones, then call that person for the number

34. An example of material that should NOT be sent by first class mail is a

    A. email copy of a letter   B. post card
    C. business reply card   D. large catalogue

35. In the operations of a government agency, a voucher is ORDINARILY used to
    A. refer someone to the agency for a position or assignment
    B. certify that an agency's records of financial trans-actions are accurate
    C. order payment from agency funds of a stated amount to an individual
    D. enter a statement of official opinion in the records of the agency

Questions 36-40.

ENGLISH USAGE

DIRECTIONS: Each question from 36 through 40 contains a sentence. Read each sentence carefully to decide whether it is correct. Then, in the space at the right, mark your answer:

(A) if the sentence is incorrect because of bad grammar or sentence structure

(B) if the sentence is incorrect because of bad punctuation

(C) if the sentence is incorrect because of bad capitalization

(D) if the sentence is correct

Each incorrect sentence has only one type of error. Consider a sentence correct if it has no errors, although there may be other correct ways of saying the same thing.

SAMPLE QUESTION I: One of our clerks were promoted yesterday.

The subject of this sentence is one, so the verb should be *was promoted* instead of *were promoted.* Since the sentence is incorrect because of bad grammar, the answer to Sample Question I is (A).

SAMPLE QUESTION II: Between you and me, I would prefer not going there.

Since this sentence is correct, the answer to Sample Question II is (D).

36. The National alliance of Businessmen is trying to persuade private businesses to hire youth in the summertime.

37. The supervisor who is on vacation, is in charge of processing vouchers.

38. The activity of the committee at its conferences is always stimulating.

39. After checking the addresses again, the letters went to the mailroom.

40. The director, as well as the employees, are interested in sharing the dividends.

Questions 41-45.

FILING

DIRECTIONS: Each question from 41 through 45 contains four names. For each question, choose the name that should be FIRST if the four names are to be arranged in alphabetical order in accordance with the Rules for Alphabetical Filing given below. Read these rules carefully. Then, for each question, indicate in the space at the right the letter before the name that should be FIRST in alphabetical order.

RULES FOR ALPHABETICAL FILING

Names of People

(1) The names of people are filed in strict alphabetical order, first according to the last name, then according to first name or initial, and finally according to middle name or initial. FOR EXAMPLE: George Allen comes before Edward Bell, and Leonard P. Reston comes before Lucille B. Reston.

(2) When last names are the same, FOR EXAMPLE, A. Green and Agnes Green, the one with the initial comes before the one with the name written out when the first initials are identical.

(3) When first and last names are alike and the middle name is given, FOR EXAMPLE, John David Doe and John Devoe Doe, the names should be filed in the alphabetical order of the middle names.

(4) When first and last names are the same, a name without a middle initial comes before one with a middle name or initial. FOR EXAMPLE, John Doe comes before both John A. Doe and John Alan Doe.

(5) When first and last names are the same, a name with a middle initial comes before one with a middle name beginning with the same initial. FOR EXAMPLE: Jack R. Hertz comes before Jack Richard Hertz.

(6) Prefixes such as De, O', Mac, Mc, and Van are filed as written and are treated as part of the names to which they are connected. FOR EXAMPLE: Robert O'Dea is filed before David Olsen.

(7) Abbreviated names are treated as if they were spelled out. FOR EXAMPLE: Chas. is filed as Charles and Thos. is filed as Thomas.

(8) Titles and designations such as Dr., Mr., and Prof, are disregarded in filing.

Names of Organizations

(1) The names of business organizations are filed according to the order in which each word in the name appears. When an organization name bears the name of a person, it is filed according to the rules for filing names of people as given above. FOR EXAMPLE: William Smith Service Co. comes before Television Distributors, Inc.

(2) Where bureau, board, office, or department appears as the first part of the title of a governmental agency, that agency should be filed under the word in the title expressing the chief function of the agency FOR EXAMPLE: Bureau of the Budget would be filed as if written Budget, (Bureau of the). The Department of Personnel would be filed as if written Personnel, (Department of).

(3) When the following words are part of an organization, they are disregarded: the, of, and.

(4) When there are numbers in a name, they are treated as if they were spelled out. FOR EXAMPLE: 10th Street Bootery is filed as Tenth Street Bootery.

SAMPLE QUESTION:
- A. Jane Earl (2)
- B. James A. Earle (4)
- C. James Earl (1)
- D. J. Earle (3)

The numbers in parentheses show the proper alphabetical order in which these names should be filed. Since the name that should be filed FIRST is James Earl, the answer to the Sample Question is (C).

41.
- A. Majorca Leather Goods
- B. Robert Maiorca and Sons
- C. Maintenance Management Corp.
- D. Majestic Carpet Mills

42.
- A. Municipal Telephone Service
- B. Municipal Reference Library
- C. Municipal Credit Union
- D. Municipal Broadcasting System

43.
- A. Robert B. Pierce
- B. R. Bruce Pierce
- C. Ronald Pierce
- D. Robert Bruce Pierce

44.
- A. Four Seasons Sports Club
- B. 14th. St. Shopping Center
- C. Forty Thieves Restaurant
- D. 42nd St. Theaters

45.
- A. Franco Franceschini
- B. Amos Franchini
- C. Sandra Franceschia
- D. Lilie Franchinesca

Questions 46-50.

SPELLING

DIRECTIONS: In each question, one of the words is misspelled. Select the letter of the misspelled word. *PRINT THE LETTER OF THE CORRECT ANSWER IN THE SPACE AT THE RIGHT.*

46.
- A. option
- B. extradite
- C. comparitive
- D. jealousy

47.
- A. handicaped
- B. assurance
- C. sympathy
- D. speech

48. A. recommend B. carraige
    C. disapprove D. independent

49. A. ingenuity   B. tenet (opinion)
    C. uncanny   D. intrigueing

50. A. arduous   B. hideous
    C. iervant   D. companies

KEY (CORRECT ANSWERS)

1. A	11. D	21. A	31. B	41. C
2. B	12. B	22. D	32. B	42. D
3. D	13. D	23. C	33. C	43. B
4. B	14. B	24. A	34. D	44. D
5. D	15. A	25. C	35. C	45. C
6. C	16. B	26. D	36. C	46. C
7. A	17. C	27. D	37. B	47. A
8. C	18. D	28. B	38. D	48. B
9. D	19. A	29. A	39. A	49. D
10. B	20. C	30. C	40. A	50. C

EXAMINATION SECTION
TEST 1

DIRECTIONS: Each question or incomplete statement is followed by several suggested answers or completions. Select the one that BEST answers the question or completes the statement. *PRINT THE LETTER OF THE CORRECT ANSWER IN THE SPACE AT THE RIGHT.*

1. Which of the following is the acceptable format for typing the date line? 1.____
   - A. 12/2/16
   - B. December 2, 2016
   - C. December 2nd, 2016
   - D. Dec. 2 2016

2. When typing a letter, which of the following is INACCURATE? 2.____
   - A. If the letter is to be more than one page long, subsequent sheets should be blank, but should match the letterhead sheet in size, color, weight, and texture.
   - B. Long quoted material must be centered and single-spaced internally.
   - C. Quotation marks must be used when there is long quoted material.
   - D. Double spacing is used above and below tables and long quotations to set them off from the rest of the material.

3. Which of the following is INACCURATE? 3.____
   - A. When an addressee's title in an inside address would overrun the center of a page, it's best to carry part of the title over to another line and to indent it by two spaces.
   - B. It is permissible to use ordinal numbers in an inside address.
   - C. In addresses involving street numbers under three, the number is written out in full.
   - D. In the inside address, suite, apartment or room numbers should be placed on the line after the street address.

4. All of the following are common styles of business letters EXCEPT 4.____
   - A. simplified
   - B. block
   - C. direct
   - D. executive

5. Please select the two choices below that correctly represent how a continuation sheet heading may be typed. 5.____
   - I. Page 2
      Mr. Alan Post
      June 25, 2016
   - II. Page 2
      Mr. Alan Post
      6-25-16
   - III. Mr. Alan Post   -2-   June 25, 2016
   - IV. Mr. Alan Post   -2-   6-25-16

   The CORRECT answer is:
   - A. I, II
   - B. II, III
   - C. I, III
   - D. II, IV

6. Which of the following is INCORRECT? It is 6.____
   - A. permissible to abbreviate honorifics in the inside address
   - B. permissible to abbreviate company or organizational names, departmental designations, or organizational titles in the inside address

C. permissible to use abbreviations in the inside address if they have been used on the printed letterhead and form part of the official company name
D. sometimes permissible to omit the colon after the salutation

7. Which of the following is INCORRECT? 7.____

   A. The subject line of a letter gives the main idea of the message as succinctly as possible.
   B. If a letter contains an enclosure, there should be a notation indicating this.
   C. Important enclosures ought to be listed numerically and described.
   D. An enclosure notation should be typed flush with the right margin.

8. Which of the following is INACCURATE about inside addresses? 8.____

   A. An intraoffice or intracompany mail stop number such as DA 3C 61B is put after the organization or company name with at least two spaces intervening.
   B. Words such as *Avenue* should not be abbreviated.
   C. With the exception of runovers, the inside address should not be more than five full lines.
   D. The inside address includes the recipient's courtesy or honorific title and his or her full name on line one; the recipient's title on the next line; the recipient's official organizational affiliation on the next line; the street address on the penultimate line; and the city, state, and zip code on the last line.

9. Which of the following is an INCORRECT example of how to copy recipients when using copy notation? 9.____

   A. cc: Martin A.Sheen
   B. cc: Ms. Connors
           Ms. Grogan
           Ms. Reynolds
   C. CC: Martin A. Sheen
   D. cc: Mr. Right
           Mr. Wrong
           Mr. Perfect

10. When typing a memo, all of the following are true EXCEPT 10.____

    A. it is permissible to use an abbreviation like 1/1/16
    B. the subject line should be underlined
    C. titles such as *Mr.* or *Dr.* are usually not used on the *To* line
    D. unless the memo is very short, paragraphs should be single-spaced and double spacing should be used to separate the paragraphs from each other

11. When typing a letter, which of the following is INACCURATE? 11.____

    A. Paragraphs in business letters are usually single-spaced, with double spacing separating them from each other.
    B. Margin settings used on subsequent sheets should match those used on the letterhead sheet.
    C. If the message contains an enumerated list, it is best to block and center the listed material by five or six more spaces, right and left.
    D. A quotation of more than three typed lines must be single-spaced and centered on the page.

12. A letter that is to be signed by Hazel Alice Putney, but written by Mary Jane Roberts, and typed by Alice Carol Bell would CORRECTLY bear the following set of initials:

    A. HAP:MJR:acb
    B. HAP:MJR:ab
    C. HAP:mjr:acb
    D. HAP:mjr:ab

13. Which of the following is INCORRECT?

    A. My dear Dr. Jones:
    B. Dear Accounting Department:
    C. Dear Dr. Jones:
    D. Dear Mr. Al Lee, Esq.:

14. Which of the following is INCORRECT?

    A. Bcc stands for blind copy or blind courtesy copy.
    B. When a blind copy is used, the notation bcc appears only on the original.
    C. When a blind copy is used, the notation may appear in the top left corner of the letterhead sheet.
    D. If following a letter style that uses indented paragraphs, the postscript should be indented in exactly the same manner.

15. All of the following are true of the complimentary close EXCEPT

    A. it is typed two lines beneath the last line of the message
    B. when using a minimal punctuation system, you may omit the comma in the complimentary close if you have used a colon in the salutation
    C. where the complimentary close is placed may vary
    D. the first word of the complimentary close is capitalized

16. When typing a letter, which of the following is INACCURATE?

    A. Tables should be centered.
    B. If the letter is to be more than one page long, at least three lines of the message itself should be carried over.
    C. The message begins two lines below the salutation in almost all letter styles.
    D. Triple spacing should be used above and below lists to set them off from the rest of the letter.

17. Which one of the following is INCORRECT?

    A. When used, special mailing instructions should be indicated on both the envelope and the letter itself.
    B. Depending upon the length of the message and the available space, special mailing instructions are usually typed flush left, about four spaces below the date line and about two lines above the first line of the inside address.
    C. Certification, registration, special delivery, and overseas air mail are all considered special mailing instructions.
    D. Special mailing instructions should not be typed in capital letters.

18. Which of the following is INCORRECT?

    A. When a letter is intended to be personal or confidential, these instructions are typewritten in capital letters on the envelope and on the letter itself.

B. When a letter is intended to be personal or confidential, these instructions are typewritten in capital letters on the envelope, but not on the letter.
C. A letter marked PERSONAL is an eyes-only communication for the recipient.
D. A letter marked CONFIDENTIAL means that the recipient and any other authorized person may open and read it.

19. All of the following are true in regard to copy notation EXCEPT

    A. when included in a letter, a copy notation should be typed flush with the left margin, two lines below the signature block or two lines below any preceding notation
    B. copy notation should appear after writer/typist initials and/or enclosure notations, if these are used
    C. the copy recipient's full name and address should be indicated
    D. if more than one individual is to be copied, recipients should be listed in alphabetical order according to full name or initials

20. When addressing envelopes, which of the following is INACCURATE?

    A. When both street address and box number are used, the destination of the letter should be placed on the line just above the city, state, and zip code line.
    B. Special mailing instructions are typed in capital letters below the postage.
    C. Special handling instructions should be typed in capital letters and underlined.
    D. The address should be single-spaced.

21. All of the following should be capitalized EXCEPT the

    A. first word of a direct quotation
    B. first word in the continuation of a split, single-sentence quotation
    C. names of organizations
    D. names of places and geographic districts, regions, divisions, and locales

22. All of the following are true about capitalization EXCEPT

    A. words indicating direction and regions are capitalized
    B. the names of rivers, seas, lakes, mountains, and oceans are capitalized
    C. the names of nationalities, tribes, languages, and races are capitalized
    D. civil, military, corporate, royal and noble, honorary, and religious titles are capitalized when they precede a name

23. All of the following are true about capitalization EXCEPT

    A. key words in the titles of musical, dramatic, artistic, and literary works are capitalized as are the first and last words
    B. the first word of the salutation and of the complimentary close of a letter is capitalized
    C. abbreviations and acronyms are not capitalized
    D. the days of the week, months of the year, holidays, and holy days are capitalized

24. All of the following are true EXCEPT

    A. an apostrophe indicates the omission of letters in contractions
    B. an apostrophe indicates the possessive case of singular and plural nouns

C. an apostrophe should not be used to indicate the omission of figures in dates
D. ellipses are used to indicate the omission of words or sentences within quoted material

25. All of the following are true EXCEPT 25.____

   A. brackets may be used to enclose words or passages in quotations to indicate the insertion of material written by someone other than the original writer
   B. brackets may be used to enclose material that is inserted within material already in parentheses
   C. a dash, rather than a colon, should be used to introduce a list
   D. a colon may be used to introduce a long quotation

26. All of the following are true EXCEPT a(n) 26.____

   A. comma may be used to set off short quotations and sayings
   B. apostrophe is often used to represent the word *per*
   C. dash may be used to indicate a sudden change or break in continuity
   D. dash may be used to set apart an emphatic or defining phrase

27. All of the following are true EXCEPT 27.____

   A. a hyphen may be used as a substitute for the word *to* between figures or words
   B. parentheses are used to enclose material that is not an essential part of the sentence and that, if not included, would not change its meaning
   C. single quotation marks are used to enclose quotations within quotations
   D. semicolons and colons are put inside closing quotation marks

28. All of the following are true EXCEPT 28.____

   A. commas and periods should be put inside closing quotation marks
   B. for dramatic effect, a semicolon may be used instead of a comma to signal longer pauses
   C. a semicolon is used to set off city and state in geographic names
   D. italics are used to represent the titles of magazines and newspapers

29. According to standard rules for typing, two spaces are left after a 29.____

   A. closing parenthesis   B. comma
   C. number   D. colon

30. All of the following are true EXCEPT 30.____

   A. rounding out large numbers is often acceptable
   B. it is best to use numerical figures to express specific hours, measures, dates, page numbers, coordinates, and addresses
   C. when a sentence begins with a number, it is best to use numerical figures rather than to spell the number out
   D. when two or more numbers appear in one sentence, it is best to spell them out consistently or use numerical figures consistently, regardless of the size of the numbers

31. All of the following are true about word division EXCEPT
    A. words should not be divided on a single letter
    B. it is acceptable to carry over two-letter endings
    C. the final word in a paragraph should not be divided
    D. words in headings should not be divided

32. All of the following are true of word division EXCEPT
    A. it is preferable to divide words of three or more syllables after the consonant
    B. it is best to avoid breaking words on more than two consecutive lines
    C. words should be divided according to pronunciation
    D. two-syllable words are divided at the end of the first syllable

33. All of the following are true of word division EXCEPT
    A. words with short prefixes should be divided after the prefix
    B. prefixes and combining forms of more than one syllable should be divided after the first syllable
    C. the following word endings are not divided: -gion, -gious, -sial, -sion, -tial, -tion, -tious, -ceous, -cial, -cient, -cion, -cious, and -geous
    D. words ending in -er should not be divided if the division could only occur on the -er form

34. All of the following are true about word division EXCEPT
    A. words should be divided so that the part of the word left at the end of the line will suggest the word
    B. abbreviations should not be divided
    C. the suffixes -able and -ible are usually divided instead of being carried over intact to the next line
    D. when the addition of -ed, -est, -er, or a similar ending causes the doubling of a final consonant, the added consonant is carried over

35. All of the following are true of word division EXCEPT
    A. words with doubled consonants are usually divided between those consonants
    B. it is permissible to divide contractions
    C. words of one syllable should not be split
    D. it is best to try to avoid divisions that add a hyphen to an already hyphenated word

36. All of the following are true of word division EXCEPT
    A. dividing proper names should be avoided wherever possible
    B. two consonants, preceded and followed by a vowel, are divided after the first consonant
    C. even though two adjoining vowels are sounded separately, it is best not to divide between the two vowels
    D. it is best not to divide the month and day when typing dates, but the year may be carried over to the next line

37. Which of the following four statements are CORRECT? It would be acceptable to divide the word
    I. *organization* after the first *a* in the word
    II. *recommend* after the first *m*
    III. *interface* between the *r* and the *f*
    IV. *development* between the *e* and the *l*
The CORRECT answer is:
    A. I *only*
    B. II, III
    C. II *only*
    D. I, II, III

38. Which of the following is divided INCORRECTLY?
    A. usu-ally
    B. call-ing
    C. pro-blem
    D. micro-computer

39. Which of the following is divided INCORRECTLY?
    A. imag-inary
    B. commun-ity
    C. manage-able
    D. commun-ion

40. Which of the following is divided INCORRECTLY?
    A. spa-ghetti
    B. retro-spective
    C. proof-reader
    D. fix-ed

41. Which of the following is divided INCORRECTLY?
    A. Mr. Han-rahan
    B. control-lable
    C. pro-jectile
    D. proj-ect

42. Which of the following is divided INCORRECTLY?
    A. prom-ise
    B. han-dling
    C. have-n't
    D. pro-duce

43. Which of the following is divided INCORRECTLY?
    A. ship-ped
    B. audi-ble
    C. hypo-crite
    D. refer-ring

44. Which of the following is divided INCORRECTLY?
    A. particu-lar
    B. spac-ious
    C. chang-ing
    D. capac-ity

45. There is a critical need to develop the ability to control the mind, especailly the ability to stop repeating negative thoughts. Often, when we must swallow our anger, we are left running an enless tape of thoughts. We can't stop thinking about what the person said and what we should have said in response. To combat this tendency, it is helpful to practice witnessing our thoughts. If we can remain detached from them, we won't fuel them, and they will just run out of gas. As we watch them, we also learn a lot about ourselves. The catch here is not to judge them. Judging may lead to selfblaming, blaming others, excuses, rationalizations, and other thoughts that just add fuel. Another technique is is substituting positive thoughts for negative ones.

8 (#1)

It is difficult to do this in the "heat of the moment". With practice, however, its possible to train the mind to do what we want it to do and to contain what we want it to contain. A mind is like a garden – we can weed it, or we can let it grow wild.
The above paragraph contains a number of typographical errors.
How many lines in this paragraph contain typographical errors?

A. 5 B. 6 C. 8 D. 9

KEY (CORRECT ANSWERS)

1. B	11. D	21. B	31. B	41. A
2. C	12. A	22. A	32. A	42. A
3. D	13. D	23. C	33. B	43. A
4. C	14. B	24. C	34. C	44. B
5. C	15. B	25. C	35. B	45. C
6. B	16. D	26. B	36. C	
7. D	17. D	27. D	37. B	
8. B	18. B	28. C	38. C	
9. D	19. C	29. D	39. B	
10. B	20. C	30. C	40. D	

TEST 2

DIRECTIONS: Each sentence may or may not contain problems in capitalization or punctuation. If there is an error, select the number of the underlined part that must be changed to make the sentence correct. If the sentence has no error, select choice E. <u>No sentence contains more than one error.</u>

1. Is the choice for <u>P</u>resident of the company<u>, George Dawson</u><u>,</u> or Marilyn Kappel<u>?</u> <u>No error</u>
   A   B   C   D   E

2. "To tell you the truth<u>,</u> I was really <u>disappointed that</u> our <u>F</u>all percentages did not show more sales growth<u>,</u>" remarked the bookkeeper. <u>No error</u>
            A   B   C   D   E

3. Bruce gave his <u>U</u>ncle clear directions to go <u>s</u>outh on Maplewood Drive<u>,</u> turn left at the intersection with Birch Lane, and then proceed for two miles until he reached Columbia <u>C</u>ounty. <u>No error</u>
                         A   B   C   D   E

4. Janet hopes to transfer to a <u>c</u>ollege in the <u>e</u>ast<u>,</u> during her <u>j</u>unior year. <u>No error</u>
                                             A   B C   D   E

5. The <u>D</u>eclaration <u>o</u>f Independence states<u>,</u> that we have the right to the pursuit of <u>H</u>appiness, but it doesn't guarantee that we'll ever find it. <u>No error</u>
             A   B   C   D   E

6. We campaigned hard for the <u>m</u>ayor<u>,</u> but we<u>'</u>re still not sure if he'll win against <u>S</u>enator Frankovich. <u>No error</u>
                                             A   B   C   D   E

7. Mr. Butler<u>'</u>s <u>F</u>ord was parked right behind <u>our's</u> on Atlantic <u>A</u>venue<u>.</u> <u>No error</u>
                    A   B   C   D   E

8. <u>"</u>I respect your opinion<u>,</u> but I cannot agree with it<u>,</u>" commented my <u>g</u>randmother. <u>No error</u>
     A   B   C   D   E

31

9. My friends, of course, were surprised when when I did so well on the Math section
    A   B   C   D
   of the test. No error
                E

10. Dr. Vogel and Senator Rydell decided that the meeting would be held on February 6,
                    A   B   C
    in Ithaca, New York. No error
       D   E

11. "Frank, do you understand what we're telling you?" asked the doctor. No error
         A   B   C   D   E

12. When I asked my daughter what she knew about politics, she claimed she
                        A   B   C
    knew nothing. No error
              D   E

13. "If you went to my high school, dad, you'd see things differently," snapped Sean.
                        A   A   B C   D
    No error
       E

14. In Carlos' third year of high school, he took geometry, psychology, french, and chemis-
         A   B   B   C   D
    try. No error
            E

15. "When you enter the building," the guard instructed us, "turn left down the long, wind-
                              A   B   C   D
    ing corridor." No error
                      E

16. We hope to spend a weekend in the Catskill Mountains in the spring, and we'd like to
                                              A   B   C   D
    go to Florida in January. No error
                                 E

17. A clerk in the department of Justice asked Carol and me if we were there on business or
         A   B   C
    just sight-seeing. No error
                    D   E

18. Jamie joined a cult, Harry's in a rock band, and Carol-Ann is studying chinese literature
                A   B   C
    at the University of Southern California. No error
           D   E

19. Parker Flash asked if my band had ever played at the
                     A
    Purple Turnip, a club in Orinoco Hills. No error
     B   C   D   E

20. "The gift of the Magi" is a short story by O'Henry that deals with the sad ironies of life.
        A B C D
    No error
     E

21. Darwin's theory was developed, as a result of his trip to the Galapagos Islands.
        A B   C   D
    No error
     E

22. Is 10 Downing street the address of Sherlock Holmes or the British Prime Minister?
         A   B   C   D
    No error
     E

23. While President Johnson was in Office, his Great Society program passed a great deal
          A   B   C   D
    of important legislation. No error
                            E

24. If, as the American Industrial Health Council's study says, one out of every five can-
      A   B   C
    cers today is caused by the workplace, it is a tragic indictment of what is happening
                                  D
    there. No error
          E

25. According to the Articles of Confederation, Congress could issue money, but it could
                                A   B   C
    not prevent States from issuing their own money. No error
               D   E

26. "I'd really like to know whos going to be shoveling the driveway this winter," said
         A   B   C   D
    Laverne. No error
             E

27. According to Carl Jung the Swiss psychologist, playing with fantasy is the key to cre-
                       A   B   C   D
    ativity. No error
             E

28. Don't you find it odd that people would prefer jumping A off the Golden Gate bridge to
        A   B
    jumping off other bridges in the area? No error
                                    C   D   E

29. While driving through the South, we saw many of the sites of famous Civil war battles.
                              A   B   C   D
    No error
    E

30. Although I have always valued my Grandmother's china, I prefer her collection
                                     A   B C
    of South American art. No error
       D   E

KEY (CORRECT ANSWERS)

1.	A	16.	E
2.	C	17.	B
3.	A	18.	C
4.	B	19.	C
5.	D	20.	A
6.	E	21.	C
7.	C	22.	B
8.	E	23.	B
9.	D	24.	D
10.	E	25.	D
11.	A	26.	B
12.	B	27.	A
13.	C	28.	B
14.	D	29.	C
15.	E	30.	A

EXAMINATION SECTION

DIRECTIONS: Each question or incomplete statement is followed by several suggested answers or completions. Select the one that BEST answers the question or completes the statement. *PRINT THE LETTER OF THE CORRECT ANSWER IN THE SPACE AT THE RIGHT.*

Questions 1-15:
For each of the following questions, PRINT on the space at the right the word TRUE if the statement is true, or FALSE if the statement is false.

1. A typist who discovers an obvious grammatical error in a report she is typing should, under ordinary circumstances, copy the material as it was given to her. 1._____

2. The initials of the typist who typed a business letter generally appear on the letter. 2._____

3. It is considered POOR letter form to have *only* the complimentary close and the signature on the second page of a business letter. 3._____

4. Correspondence which is filed according to dates of letters is said to be filed chronologically. 4._____

5. It is *usually* unnecessary to proofread punctuation marks in a report. 5._____

6. The use of window envelopes *reduces* probability of mailing a letter to the wrong address. 6._____

7. Letter size paper is *usually* longer than legal size paper. 7._____

8. It is considered GOOD typing form to have two spaces following a comma. 8._____

9. Both sheets of a two-page typed letter MUST be letterheads. 9._____

10. Before removing a typed letter from the typewriter, the typist should read the copy so that corrections may be made neatly. 10._____

11. When alphabetizing names, you should ALWAYS disregard first names. 11._____

12. When filing a large number of cards according to the name on each card, it is generally a *good* procedure to alphabetize the cards FIRST. 12._____

13. When a report may be filed in a subject file under two headings, it is *good* practice to make a cross reference. 13._____

14. If an essential point has been omitted in a business letter, it is usually considered *good* letter form to include this point in a brief postscript.

14._____

15. Rough draft copies of a report should generally be single-spaced.

15._____

Questions 16-22:
The following items consist of problems in arithmetic. Print in the space at the right the word TRUE if the statement is true, and FALSE if the statement is false.

16. If the rate for first-class mail is 37 cents for each ounce or fraction of an ounce and 23 cents for each ounce or fraction of an ounce above one ounce, then the total cost of sending by first-class mail three letters weighing 1-1/2 ounces, 2 ounces, and 2-1/2 ounces, respectively, would be $1.80.

16._____

17. A typist, who in one hour typed a report consisting of five pages with 60 lines per page and 10 words per line, would have typed at the rate of 45 words per minute.

17._____

18. If a department store employs 45 clerks, 21 typists, and 18 stenographers, the percentage of these employees who are typists is 25%.

18._____

19. If four typists, who type at the same rate of speed, type 1,000 letters in 12 hours, then it will take six typists nine hours to type 1,000 letters.

19._____

20. If 15% of a stenographer's time is spent in taking dictation and 45% of her time is taken up in transcribing her notes, then she has a remainder of two-fifths of her time for performing other duties.

20._____

21. A typist completed 14 pages of a 24-page report before being asked to speak briefly with her employer, then typed the remaining 10 pages. Up until the time she spoke with her employer, the typist had already completed approximately 58% of the report.

21._____

22. Employee A types at a rate of 48 words per minute, while Employee B types at a rate of 54 words per minute. If both employees spend exactly 2-1/4 hours typing reports, Employee B will have typed approximately 810 more words than Employee A.

22._____

Questions 23-54:
Each of the following items consists of two words preceded by the letters A and B. In each item, *one* of the words may be spelled INCORRECTLY, or *both* words may be spelled CORRECTLY. If one of the words is spelled incorrectly, print in the space at the right the letter corresponding to the incorrect word. If both are spelled correctly, print the answer C.

23. A. accessible	B. artifical	23._____
24. A. feild	B. arranged	24._____
25. A. admittence	B. hastily	25._____
26. A. easely	B. readily	26._____
27. A. pursue	B. decend	27._____
28. A. measure	B. laboratory	28._____
29. A. exausted	B. traffic	29._____
30. A. discussion	B. unpleasant	30._____
31. A. campaign	B. murmer	31._____
32. A. guarantee	B. sanatary	32._____
33. A. communication	B. safty	33._____
34. A. numerus	B. celebration	34._____
35. A. nourish	B. begining	35._____
36. A. courious	B. witness	36._____
37. A. undoubtedly	B. thoroughly	37._____
38. A. justified	B. offering	38._____
39. A. predjudice	B. license	39._____
40. A. label	B. pamphlet	40._____
41. A. bulletin	B. physical	41._____
42. A. assure	B. exceed	42._____
43. A. advantagous	B. evident	43._____

44. A. benefit   B. occured   44. _____

45. A. acquire   B. graditude   45. _____

46. A. amenable   B. boundry   46. _____

47. A. deceive   B. voluntary   47. _____

48. A. imunity   B. conciliate   48. _____

49. A. acknoledge   B. presume   49. _____

50. A. substitute   B. prespiration   50. _____

51. A. reputible   B. announce   51. _____

52. A. luncheon   B. wretched   52. _____

53. A. regrettable   B. proficiency   53. _____

54. A. rescind   B. dissappoint   54. _____

Questions 55-72:
Each of the sentences that follow may be classified MOST appropriately under one of the following three categories:
    A. *faulty* because of incorrect grammar
    B. *faulty* because of incorrect punctuation
    C. *correct*

Examine each sentence, then select the best answer as listed above and place the letter in the space at the right. All incorrect sentences contain only ONE type of error. Consider a sentence correct if it contains none of the types of errors mentioned, even though there may be other correct ways of expressing the same thought.

55. He sent the notice to the clerk who hired you yesterday.   55. _____

56. It must be admitted, however that you were not informed of this change.   56. _____

57. Only the employees who have served in this grade for at least two years are eligible for promotion.   57. _____

58. The work was divided equally between she and Mary.   58. _____

59. He thought that you were not available at the time.   59. _____

60. When the messenger returns; please give him this package.   60. _____

61. The new secretary prepared, typed, addressed, and delivered, the notices. 61. _____

62. Walking into the room, his desk can be seen at the rear. 62. _____

63. Although John has worked here longer then she, he produces a smaller amount of work. 63. _____

64. She said she could of typed this report yesterday. 64. _____

65. Neither one of these procedures are adequate for the efficient performance of this task. 65. _____

66. The typewriter is the tool of the typist; the cash register, the tool of the cashier. 66. _____

67. "The assignment must be completed as soon as possible" said the supervisor. 67. _____

68. As you know, office handbooks are issued to all new employees. 68. _____

69. Writing a speech is sometimes easier than to deliver it before an audience. 69. _____

70. Mr. Brown our accountant, will audit the accounts next week. 70. _____

71. Give the assignment to whomever is able to do it most efficiently. 71. _____

72. The supervisor expected either your or I to file these reports. 72. _____

Questions 73-90:
For each of the following test items, print the letter in the space at the right of the answer that BEST completes the statement.

73. A PREVALENT practice is one which is 73. _____
    A. rare   B. unfair   C. widespread   D. correct

74. To prepare a RECAPITULATION means *most nearly* to prepare a 74. _____
    A. summary   B. revision   C. defense   D. decision

75. An ADVERSE decision is one which is 75. _____
    A. unfavorable   B. unwise
    C. anticipated   D. backwards

76. A COMMENDATORY report is one which 76. _____
    A. expresses praise   B. contains contradictions
    C. is too detailed   D. is threatening

77. "The council will DEFER action on this matter." The word DEFER means *most nearly*
    A. hasten B. consider C. postpone D. reject

78. MEAGER results are those which are
    A. satisfactory B. scant
    C. unexpected D. praiseworthy

79. An ARDUOUS job assignment
    A. requires much supervision B. is laborious
    C. absorbs one's interest D. is lengthy

80. "This employee was IMPLICATED." The word IMPLICATED *most nearly* means
    A. demoted B. condemned C. involved D. accused

81. To be DETAINED means *most nearly* to be
    A. entertained B. held back
    C. sent away D. scolded

82. An AMIABLE person is one who is
    A. active B. pleasing C. thrifty D. foolish

83. A UNIQUE procedure is one which is
    A. simple B. uncommon C. useless D. ridiculous

84. The word REPLENISH means *most nearly* to
    A. give up B. punish C. refill D. empty

85. A CONCISE report is one which is
    A. logical B. favorable C. brief D. intelligent

86. ELATED means *most nearly*
    A. lengthened B. matured C. excited D. youthful

87. SANCTION means *most nearly*
    A. approval B. delay C. priority D. veto

88. EGOTISTIC means *most nearly*
    A. tiresome B. self-centered
    C. sly D. smartly attired

89. TRITE means *most nearly*
    A. brilliant B. unusual
    C. funny D. commonplace

90. FESTIVE means *most nearly*
    A. edible B. joyous C. proud D. serene

KEY (CORRECT ANSWERS)

1. F	31. B	61. B
2. T	32. B	62. A
3. T	33. B	63. C
4. T	34. A	64. A
5. F	35. B	65. A
6. T	36. A	66. C
7. F	37. C	67. B
8. F	38. C	68. C
9. F	39. A	69. A
10. T	40. C	70. B
11. F	41. C	71. A
12. T	42. C	72. A
13. T	43. A	73. C
14. F	44. B	74. A
15. F	45. B	75. A
16. F	46. B	76. A
17. F	47. C	77. C
18. T	48. A	78. B
19. F	49. A	79. B
20. T	50. B	80. C
21. T	51. A	81. B
22. T	52. C	82. B
23. B	53. C	83. B
24. A	54. B	84. C
25. A	55. A	85. C
26. A	56. B	86. C
27. B	57. C	87. A
28. C	58. A	88. B
29. A	59. C	89. D
30. C	60. B	90. B

EXAMINATION SECTION
TEST 1

DIRECTIONS: Each question or incomplete statement is followed by several suggested answers or completions. Select the one that BEST answers the question or completes the statement. *PRINT THE LETTER OF THE CORRECT ANSWER IN THE SPACE AT THE RIGHT.*

1. A coworker has e-mailed a file containing a spreadsheet for your review. Which of the following programs will open the file?   1.____

   A. Adobe Reader
   B. Microsoft Excel
   C. Microsoft PowerPoint
   D. Adobe Illustrator

2. A report needs to be forwarded immediately to a supervisor in another office. Which of the following is the LEAST effective way of giving the supervisor the report?   2.____

   A. scanning the report and e-mailing the file
   B. faxing it to the supervisor's office
   C. uploading it to the office network and informing the supervisor
   D. waiting for the supervisor to come to your office and giving it to him/her then

3. Suppose your supervisor is on the telephone in his office and an applicant arrives for a scheduled interview with him.
   Of the following, the BEST procedure to follow ordinarily is to   3.____

   A. informally chat with the applicant in your office until your supervisor has finished his phone conversation
   B. escort him directly into your supervisor's office and have him wait for him there
   C. inform your supervisor of the applicant's arrival and try to make the applicant feel comfortable while waiting
   D. have him hang up his coat and tell him to go directly in to see your supervisor

Questions 4-9.

DIRECTIONS: Questions 4 through 9 each consist of a sentence which may or may not be an example of good English usage. Consider grammar, punctuation, spelling, capitalization, awkwardness, etc. Examine each sentence, and then choose the correct statement about it from the four choices below it. If the English usage in the sentence given is better than any of the changes suggested in options B, C, or D, choose option A. Do not choose an option that will change the meaning of the sentence.

4. The report, along with the accompanying documents, were submitted for review.   4.____

   A. This is an example of acceptable writing.
   B. The words *were submitted* should be changed to *was submitted*.
   C. The word *accompanying* should be spelled *accompaning*.
   D. The comma after the word *report* should be taken out.

5. If others must use your files, be certain that they understand how the system works, but insist that you do all the filing and refiling.   5._____

   A. This is an example of acceptable writing.
   B. There should be a period after the word *works*, and the word *but* should start a new sentence.
   C. The words *filing* and *refiling* should be spelled *fileing* and *refileing*.
   D. There should be a comma after the word *but*.

6. The appeal was not considered because of its late arrival.   6._____

   A. This is an example of acceptable writing.
   B. The word *its* should be changed to *it's*.
   C. The word *its* should be changed to *the*.
   D. The words *late arrival* should be changed to *arrival late*.

7. The letter must be read carefuly to determine under which subject it should be filed.   7._____

   A. This is an example of acceptable writing.
   B. The word *under* should be changed to *at*.
   C. The word *determine* should be spelled *determin*.
   D. The word *carefuly* should be spelled *carefully*.

8. He showed potential as an office manager, but he lacked skill in delegating work.   8._____

   A. This is an example of acceptable writing.
   B. The word *delegating* should be spelled *delagating*.
   C. The word *potential* should be spelled *potencial*.
   D. The words *lie lacked* should be changed to *was lacking*.

9. His supervisor told him that it would be all right to receive personal mail at the office.   9._____

   A. This is an example of acceptable writing.
   B. The words *all right* should be changed to *alright*.
   C. The word *personal* should be spelled *personel*.
   D. The word *mail* should be changed to *letters*.

Questions 10-13.

DIRECTIONS: Questions 10 through 13 are to be answered SOLELY on the basis of the information given in the following passage.

Typed pages can reflect the simplicity of modern art in a machine age. Lightness and evenness can be achieved by proper layout and balance of typed lines and white space. Instead of solid, cramped masses of uneven, crowded typing, there should be a pleasing balance up and down as well as horizontal.

To have real balance, your page must have a center. The eyes see the center of the sheet slightly above the real center. This is the way both you and the reader see it. Try imagining a line down the center of the page that divides the paper in equal halves. On either side of your paper, white space and blocks of typing need to be similar in size and shape. Although left and right margins should be equal, top and bottom margins need not be as exact. It looks better to hold a bottom border wider than a top margin, so that your typing rests *upon a cushion of white space. To add interest to the appearance of the page, try making one paragraph between one-half and two-thirds the size of an adjacent paragraph.*

Thus, by taking full advantage of your typewriter, the pages that you type will not only be accurate but will also be attractive.

10. It can be inferred from the passage that the BASIC importance of proper balancing on a typed page is that proper balancing

    A. makes a typed page a work of modern art
    B. provides exercise in proper positioning of a typewriter
    C. increases the amount of typed copy on the paper
    D. draws greater attention and interest to the page

11. A reader will tend to see the center of a typed page

    A. somewhat higher than the true center
    B. somewhat lower than the true center
    C. on either side of the true center
    D. about two-thirds of an inch above the true center

12. Which of the following suggestions is NOT given by the passage?

    A. Bottom margins may be wider than top borders.
    B. Keep all paragraphs approximately the same size.
    C. Divide your page with an imaginary line down the middle.
    D. Side margins should be equalized.

13. Of the following, the BEST title for this passage is:

    A. INCREASING THE ACCURACY OF THE TYPED PAGE
    B. DETERMINATION OF MARGINS FOR TYPED COPY
    C. LAYOUT AND BALANCE OF THE TYPED PAGE
    D. HOW TO TAKE FULL ADVANTAGE OF THE TYPEWRITER

14. In order to type addresses on a large number of envelopes MOST efficiently, you should

    A. insert another envelope into the typewriter before removing each typed envelope
    B. take each typed envelope out of the machine before starting the next envelope
    C. insert several envelopes into the machine at one time, keeping all top and bottom edges even
    D. insert several envelopes into the machine at one time, keeping the top edge of each envelope two inches below the top edge of the one beneath it

15. A senior typist has completed copying a statistical report from a rough draft. Of the following, the BEST way to be sure that her typing is correct is for the typist to

    A. fold the rough draft, line it up with the typed copy, compare one-half of the columns with the original, and have a co-worker compare the other half
    B. check each line of the report as it is typed and then have a co-worker check each line again after the entire report is finished

C. have a co-worker add each column and check the totals on the typed copy with the totals on the original
D. have a co-worker read aloud from the rough draft while the typist checks the typed copy and then have the typist read while the co-worker checks

16. In order to center a heading when typing a report, you should 16.___

    A. measure your typing paper with a ruler and begin the heading one-third of the way in from the left margin
    B. begin the heading at the point on the typewriter scale which is 50 minus the number of letters in the heading
    C. multiply the number of characters in the heading by two and begin the heading that number of spaces in from the left margin
    D. begin the heading at the point on the scale which is equal to the center point of your paper minus one-half the number of characters and spaces in the heading

17. Which of the following recommendations concerning the use of copy paper for making typewritten copies should NOT be followed? 17.___

    A. Copy papers should be checked for wrinkles before being used.
    B. Legal-size copy paper may be folded if it is too large to fit into a convenient drawer space.
    C. When several sheets of paper are being used, they should be fastened with a paper clip at the top after insertion in the typewriter.
    D. For making many copies, paper of the same weight and brightness should be used.

18. Assume that a new typist, Norma Garcia, has been assigned to work under your supervision and is reporting to work for the first time. You formally introduce Norma to her co-workers and suggest that a few of the other typists explain the office procedures and typing formats to her. The practice of instructing Norma in her duties in this manner is 18.___

    A. *good* because she will be made to feel at home
    B. *good* because she will learn more about routine office tasks from co-workers than from you
    C. *poor* because her co-workers will resent the extra work
    D. *poor* because you will not have enough control over her training

19. Suppose that Jean Brown, a typist, is typing a letter following the same format that she has always used. However, she notices that the other two typists in her office are also typing letters, but are using a different format. Jean is concerned that she might not have been informed of a change in format. 19.___
Of the following, the FIRST action that Jean should take is to

    A. seek advice from her supervisor as to which format to use
    B. ask the other typists whether she should use a new format for typing letters
    C. disregard the format that the other typists are using and continue to type in the format she had been using
    D. use the format that the other typists are using, assuming that it is a newly accepted method

20. Suppose that the new office to which you have been assigned has put up Christmas decorations, and a Christmas party is being planned by the city agency in which you work. However, nothing has been said about Christmas gifts.
It would be CORRECT for you to assume that

    A. you are expected to give a gift to your supervisor
    B. your supervisor will give you a gift
    C. you are expected to give gifts only to your subordinates
    D. you will neither receive gifts nor will you be expected to give any

20.____

KEY (CORRECT ANSWERS)

1.	B	11.	A
2.	D	12.	B
3.	C	13.	C
4.	B	14.	A
5.	A	15.	D
6.	A	16.	D
7.	D	17.	B
8.	A	18.	D
9.	A	19.	A
10.	D	20.	D

TEST 2

DIRECTIONS: Each question or incomplete statement is followed by several suggested answers or completions. Select the one that BEST answers the question or completes the statement. *PRINT THE LETTER OF THE CORRECT ANSWER IN THE SPACE AT THE RIGHT.*

1. The supervisor you assist is under great pressure to meet certain target dates. He has scheduled an emergency meeting to take place in a few days, and he asks you to send out notices immediately. As you begin to prepare the notices, however, you realize he has scheduled the meeting for a Saturday, which is not a working day. Also, you sense that your supervisor is not in a good mood.
Which of the following is the MOST effective method of handling this situation?

   A. Change the meeting date to the first working day after that Saturday and send out the notices.
   B. Change the meeting date to a working day on which his calendar is clear and send out the notices.
   C. Point out to your supervisor that the date is a Saturday.
   D. Send out the notices as they are since you have received specific instructions.

1._____

Questions 2-7.

DIRECTIONS: Questions 2 through 7 each consist of a sentence which may or may not be an example of good English usage. Consider grammar, punctuation, spelling, capitalization, awkwardness, etc. Examine each sentence, and then choose the correct statement about it from the four choices below it. If the English usage in the sentence given is better than any of the changes suggested in options B, C, or D, choose option A. Do not choose an option that will change the meaning of the sentence.

2. The typist used an extention cord in order to connect her typewriter to the outlet nearest to her desk.

   A. This is an example of acceptable writing.
   B. A period should be placed after the word *cord,* and the word *in* should have a capital I.
   C. A comma should be placed after the word *typewriter.*
   D. The word *extention* should be spelled *extension.*

2._____

3. He would have went to the conference if he had received an invitation.

   A. This is an example of acceptable writing.
   B. The word *went* should be replaced by the word *gone.*
   C. The word *had* should be replaced by *would have.*
   D. The word *conference* should be spelled *conferance.*

3._____

4. In order to make the report neater, he spent many hours rewriting it.

   A. This is an example of acceptable writing.
   B. The word *more* should be inserted before the word *neater.*
   C. There should be a colon after the word *neater.*
   D. The word *spent* should be changed to *have spent.*

4._____

5. His supervisor told him that he should of read the memorandum more carefully.   5._____

    A. This is an example of acceptable writing.
    B. The word *memorandum* should be spelled *memorandom*.
    C. The word *of* should be replaced by the word *have*.
    D. The word *carefully* should be replaced by the word *careful*.

6. It was decided that two separate reports should be written.   6._____

    A. This is an example of acceptable writing.
    B. A comma should be inserted after the word *decided*.
    C. The word *be* should be replaced by the word *been*.
    D. A colon should be inserted after the word *that*.

7. She don't seem to understand that the work must be done as soon as possible.   7._____

    A. This is an example of acceptable writing.
    B. The word *doesn't* should replace the word *don't*.
    C. The word *why* should replace the word *that*.
    D. The word *as* before the word *soon* should be eliminated.

Questions 8-11.

DIRECTIONS: Questions 8 through 11 are to be answered SOLELY on the basis of the following passage.

There is nothing that will take the place of good sense on the part of the stenographer. You may be perfect in transcribing exactly what the dictator says and your speed may be adequate; but without an understanding of the dictator's intent as well as his words, you are likely to be a mediocre secretary.

A serious error that is made when taking dictation is putting down something that does not make sense. Most people who dictate material would rather be asked to repeat and explain than to receive transcribed material which has errors due to inattention or doubt. Many dictators request that their grammar be corrected by their secretaries; but unless specifically asked to do so, secretaries should not do it without first checking with the dictator. Secretaries should be aware that, in some cases, dictators may use incorrect grammar or slang expressions to create a particular effect.

Some people dictate commas, periods, and paragraphs, while others expect the stenographer to know when, where, and how to punctuate. A well-trained secretary should be able to indicate the proper punctuation by listening to the pauses and tones of the dictator's voice.

A stenographer who has taken dictation from the same person for a period of time should be able to understand him under most conditions. By increasing her tact, alertness, and efficiency, a secretary can become more competent.

8. According to the passage, which of the following statements concerning the dictation of punctuation is CORRECT?   8._____
A

    A. dictator may use incorrect punctuation to create a desired style

B. dictator should indicate all punctuation
C. stenographer should know how to punctuate based on the pauses and tones of the dictator
D. stenographer should not type any punctuation if it has not been dictated to her

9. According to the passage, how should secretaries handle grammatical errors in a dictation?
Secretaries should

   A. *not correct* grammatical errors unless the dictator is aware that this is being done
   B. *correct* grammatical errors by having the dictator repeat the line with proper pauses
   C. *correct* grammatical errors if they have checked the correctness in a grammar book
   D. *correct* grammatical errors based on their own good sense

10. If a stenographer is confused about the method of spacing and indenting of a report which has just been dictated to her, she GENERALLY should

   A. do the best she can
   B. ask the dictator to explain what she should do
   C. try to improve her ability to understand dictated material
   D. accept the fact that her stenographic ability is not adequate

11. In the last line of the first paragraph, the word *mediocre* means MOST NEARLY

   A. superior
   B. disregarded
   C. respected
   D. second-rate

12. Assume that is is your responsibility to schedule meetings for your supervisor, who believes in starting these meetings strictly on time. He has told you to schedule separate meetings with Mr. Smith and Ms. Jones, which will last approximately 20 minutes each. You have told Mr. Smith to arrive at 10:00 A.M. and Ms. Jones at 10:30 A.M. Your supervisor will have an hour of free time at 11:00 A.M. At 10:25 A.M., Mr. Smith arrives and states that there was a train delay, and he is sorry that he is late. Ms. Jones has not yet arrived. You do not know who Mr. Smith and Ms. Jones are or what the meetings will be about.
Of the following, the BEST course of action for you to take is to

   A. send Mr. Smith in to see your supervisor; and when Ms. Jones arrives, tell her that your supervisor's first meeting will take more time than he expected
   B. tell Mr. Smith that your supervisor has a meeting at 10:30 A.M. and that you will have to reschedule his meeting for another day
   C. check with your supervisor to find out if he would prefer to see Mr. Smith immediately or at 11:00 A.M.
   D. encourage your supervisor to meet with Mr. Smith immediately because Mr. Smith's late arrival was not intentional

13. Assume that you have been told by your boss not to let anyone disturb him for the rest of the afternoon unless absolutely necessary since he has to complete some urgent work. His supervisor, who is the bureau chief, telephones and asks to speak to him.
The BEST course of action for you to take is to

A. ask the bureau chief if he can leave a message
B. ask your boss if he can take the call
C. tell the bureau chief that your boss is out
D. tell your boss that his instructions will get you into trouble

14. Which one of the following is the MOST advisable procedure for a stenographer to follow when a dictator asks her to make extra copies of dictated material?

    A. Note the number of copies required at the beginning of the notes.
    B. Note the number of copies required at the end of the notes.
    C. Make a mental note of the number of copies required to be made.
    D. Make a checkmark beside the notes to serve as a reminder that extra copies are required.

15. Suppose that, as you are taking shorthand notes, the dictator tells you that the sentence he has just dictated is to be deleted.
    Of the following, the BEST thing for you to do is to

    A. place the correction in the left-hand margin next to the deleted sentence
    B. write the word *delete* over the sentence and place the correction on a separate page for corrections
    C. erase the sentence and use that available space for the correction
    D. draw a line through the sentence and begin the correction on the next available line

16. Assume that your supervisor, who normally dictates at a relatively slow rate, begins dictating to you very rapidly. You find it very difficult to keep up at this speed. Which one of the following is the BEST action to take in this situation?

    A. Ask your supervisor to dictate more slowly since you are having difficulty.
    B. Continue to take the dictation at the fast speed and fill in the blanks later.
    C. Interrupt your supervisor with a question about the dictation, hoping that when she begins again it will be slower.
    D. Refuse to take the dictation unless given at the speed indicated in your job description.

17. Assume that you have been asked to put a heading on the second, third, and fourth pages of a four-page letter to make sure they can be identified in case they are separated from the first page.
    Which of the following is it LEAST important to include in such a heading?

    A. Date of the letter
    B. Initials of the typist
    C. Name of the person to whom the letter is addressed
    D. Number of the page

18. Which one of the following is NOT generally accepted when dividing words at the end of a line?
    Dividing

    A. a hyphenated word at the hyphen
    B. a word immediately after the prefix
    C. a word immediately before the suffix
    D. proper names between syllables

19. In the preparation of a business letter which has two enclosures, the MOST generally accepted of the following procedures to follow is to type

    A. *See Attached Items* one line below the last line of the body of the letter
    B. *See Attached Enclosures* to the left of the signature
    C. *Enclosures 2* at the left margin below the signature line
    D. nothing on the letter to indicate enclosures since it will be obvious to the reader that there are enclosures in the envelope

20. Standard rules for typing spacing have developed through usage. According to these rules, one space is left AFTER

    A. a comma
    B. every sentence
    C. a colon
    D. an opening parenthesis

KEY (CORRECT ANSWERS)

1.	C	11.	D
2.	D	12.	C
3.	B	13.	B
4.	A	14.	A
5.	C	15.	D
6.	A	16.	A
7.	B	17.	B
8.	C	18.	D
9.	A	19.	C
10.	B	20.	A

EXAMINATION SECTION
TEST 1

DIRECTIONS: Each question or incomplete statement is followed by several suggested answers or completions. Select the one that BEST answers the question or completes the statement. *PRINT THE LETTER OF THE CORRECT ANSWER IN THE SPACE AT THE RIGHT.*

ABBREVIATIONS

DIRECTIONS: In the following groups, only one definition of the abbreviation is correct. Indicate the letter of the CORRECT definition.

1. circa
   - A. circumference
   - B. circle
   - C. at or near a given date
   - D. circulation

2. ibid.
   - A. that is
   - B. for the same reason
   - C. for example
   - D. the same reference as the one immediately preceding

3. op. cit.
   - A. operation cited
   - B. the same work as one previously mentioned
   - C. operas mentioned
   - D. open citation

4. B/L
   - A. bill of lading
   - B. barrel loadings
   - C. built by law
   - D. borrowed or loaned

5. cf.
   - A. counterfeit
   - B. compare
   - C. chief
   - D. cold and fair

6. et al.
   - A. eat everything
   - B. and/or
   - C. and others
   - D. and so forth

7. f.
   - A. false
   - B. page following
   - C. free
   - D. fund

8. id.
   - A. ideas
   - B. in debt
   - C. the same
   - D. idle

55

9. sic.

   A. ill
   B. said in court
   C. sealed in court
   D. thus

10. v.

   A. by way of
   B. vintage
   C. for
   D. versus

11.

   A. end of game
   B. exactly as guaranteed
   C. that is
   D. for example

12. M

   A. 500   B. 1000   C. 50   D. 100

13. stet

   A. stated
   B. streets
   C. let it stand
   D. stationery

14. u.c.

   A. ukase
   B. upper case
   C. under consideration
   D. under control

15. HCL

   A. high cost of living
   B. hydrochloric oxide
   C. head, chest, and limbs
   D. hold courts of law

KEY (CORRECT ANSWERS)

1. C
2. D
3. B
4. A
5. B

6. C
7. B
8. C
9. D
10. D

11. D
12. B
13. C
14. B
15. A

TEST 2

BUSINESS INFORMATION

DIRECTIONS: In the following groups, only one answer is correct. Indicate the CORRECT answer.

1. Ball point, dotted line, wheel, dash line wheel, and wire loop all refer to different types of

    A. pens
    B. stapling machines
    C. styli
    D. mechanical pencils

2. The CORRECT salutation for a letter with an *Attention* line is

    A. Gentlemen
    B. Dear Sir
    C. Dear Madam
    D. Dear Mr. Blank

3. To indicate that a copy of a letter is being sent to a person other than the addressee, it is BEST to

    A. include this information in the body of the letter
    B. omit this information
    C. indicate this information as a postscript
    D. type the letters *CC* and the name of the person under the identifying initials

4. To type CO_2 or X^2 properly, you should use the

    A. carriage return lever
    B. ratchet release
    C. variable line spacer
    D. line space regulator

5. With a pica typewriter, the number of horizontal spaces on paper 8 1/2 inches wide is

    A. 80 B. 85 C. 100 D. 102

6. The Macintosh Computer is manufactured by

    A. Unisys B. Tandem C. IBM D. Apple

7. The only machine listed below which is NOT a liquid duplicator is

    A. mimeograph B. ditto C. xerox D. offset

8. Three of the following words describe the same part of the typewriter. Indicate which does NOT belong with the others.

    A. Bail B. Platen C. Roller D. Cylinder

9. The part of the typewriter NOT on the carriage is the

    A. paper guide
    B. ribbon selector
    C. carriage release lever
    D. variable line spacer

10. Indicate which one of the following statements is NOT true.
    In a business letter,

    A. the date may be pivoted, centered, or typed at the left margin
    B. the firm name is typed with solid capital letters
    C. there must be a comma after the complimentary close
    D. the typist's initials may be typed with small letters or capital letters

11. Indicate which one of the following statements concerning the NOMA Simplified Letter Style is NOT true:
    The

    A. extreme block form is used
    B. date is omitted
    C. salutation is omitted
    D. complimentary close is omitted

11.____

12. One of the following letter styles is MOST difficult to type and, therefore, takes more time to type. Indicate which style it is.

    A. Hanging indention   B. Semi-block
    C. Inverted address   D. Simplified (NOMA)

12.____

13. Indicate which one of the following statements is TRUE. There is(are) always

    A. one space after a semicolon
    B. one space after a colon
    C. two spaces after a period
    D. two spaces after a question mark

13.____

14. When a letter is folded into a #10 envelope, there are _____ creases.

    A. 2   B. 4   C. 3   D. 5

14.____

15. Which one of the following statements concerning position and posture at the typewriter is INCORRECT?

    A. Your arms and elbows should be hanging loosely.
    B. The heel of the hand should rest comfortably on the frame of the typewriter for support.
    C. Your back should be erect so that you can sit up tall.
    D. Your feet should be kept flat on the floor.

15.____

KEY (CORRECT ANSWERS)

1. C
2. A
3. D
4. B
5. B

6. D
7. C
8. A
9. B
10. C

11. B
12. A
13. A
14. A
15. B

———

TEST 3

LITERATURE

DIRECTIONS: One title in each lettered group does NOT belong with the others. Indicate the letter of the INCORRECT title in each group.

1. Books dealing with Africa:

    A. ALBERT SCHWEITZER by Joseph Gollomb
    B. TO KILL A MOCKINGBIRD by Harper Lee
    C. CRY, THE BELOVED COUNTRY by Alan Paton
    D. WHITE WITCH DOCTOR by L.A. Stinetorf

    1.____

2. Books dealing with Americans all:

    A. MAMA'S BANK ACCOUNT by Kathryn Forbes
    B. MY NAME IS ARAM by William Saroyan
    C. PENDENNIS by William Thackeray
    D. ANYTHING CAN HAPPEN by George and Helen Papashvily

    2.____

3. Books dealing with artists:

    A. THE LEOPARD by Giuseppe di Lampedusa
    B. PAINTBOX SUMMER by Betty Cavanna
    C. HEADS AND TALES by Malvina Hoffman
    D. GRANDMA MOSES, MY LIFE HISTORY by A.M. Moses

    3.____

4. Books dealing with ballet:

    A. ALICIA MARKOVA: HER LIFE AND ART by Anton Dolin
    B. MOIRA SHEARER by Pigeon Crowle
    C. DANCE TO THE PIPER by Agnes DeMille
    D. THE PIT by Frank Norris

    4.____

5. Books dealing with courageous Blacks:

    A. THE JACKIE ROBINSON STORY by A.W. Mann
    B. DR. GEORGE WASHINGTON CARVER by Shirley Graham and G.D. Lipscomb
    C. THE GREEN PASTURES by Marc Connelly
    D. THE RED AND THE BLACK by Stendhal

    5.____

6. Books dealing with dating:

    A. HUGHIE by Eugene O'Neill
    B. JUNIOR MISS by Sally Benson
    C. SEVENTEENTH SUMMER by Maureen Daly
    D. OUR TOWN by Thornton Wilder

    6.____

7. Books dealing with doctors:

    A. ARROWSMITH by Sinclair Lewis
    B. KINGSBLOOD ROYAL by Sinclair Lewis
    C. BURMA SURGEON by G.S. Seagrave
    D. THE CITADEL by A.J. Cronin

    7.____

8. Books dealing with dogs: 8._____

    A. MY FRIEND FLICKA by Mary O'Hara
    B. THE CALL OF THE WILD by Jack London
    C. THE VOICE OF BUGLE ANN by MacKinlay Kantor
    D. SILVER CHIEF by Jack O'Brien

9. Books dealing with the French Revolution: 9._____

    A. THE SCARLET PIMPERNEL by Emmuska Orczy
    B. A TALE OF TWO CITIES by Charles Dickens
    C. THE GREENGAGE SUMMER by Rumer Godden
    D. DESIREE by Annemarie Selinko

10. Books dealing with animal tales: 10._____

    A. WINNIE-THE-POOH by A.A. Milne
    B. BAMBI by Felix Salten
    C. CHARLOTTE'S WEB by E.B. White
    D. THE ANIMAL KINGDOM by Philip Barry

11. Books dealing with music: 11._____

    A. INTERRUPTED MELODY by Marjorie Lawrence
    B. REBECCA by Daphne DuMaurier
    C. ENCHANTING JENNY LIND by Laura Benet
    D. STORY OF THE TRAPP FAMILY SINGERS by M.A. Trapp

12. Books dealing with sports: 12._____

    A. WITH ROCKNE AT NOTRE DAME by Gene Schoor
    B. THE RED PONY by John Steinbeck
    C. COLLEGE SLUGGER by E.E. Fitzgerald
    D. THE KID WHO BATTED 1.000 by Bob Allison and F.E. Hill

13. Books dealing with the theater: 13._____

    A. THE SEARCH by C.P. Snow
    B. WITH A FEATHER ON MY NOSE by Billie Burke
    C. A STAR DANCED by Gertrude Lawrence
    D. AT 33 by Eva LeGallienne

14. Books dealing with World War II: 14._____

    A. THE MOON IS DOWN by John Steinbeck
    B. A FAREWELL TO ARMS by Ernest Hemingway
    C. COMMAND DECISION by W.W. Haines
    D. INTO THE VALLEY by John Hersey

15. Books dealing with science fiction: 15._____

    A. SPACE CADET by R.A. Heinlein
    B. THE DOOMED OASIS by Hammond Innes
    C. STAR MAN'S SON by Andre Norton
    D. HUMANOIDS by Jack Williamson

KEY (CORRECT ANSWERS)

1. B
2. C
3. A
4. D
5. D

6. A
7. B
8. A
9. C
10. D

11. B
12. B
13. A
14. B
15. B

TEST 4

PRONUNCIATION

DIRECTIONS: In the following groups, one pronunciation is incorrect. Indicate the letter of the INCORRECT pronunciation. Listed next to each word is the pronunciation. The accented syllable is indicated by capital letters.

1. A. abdomen - ab DOE men
   B. aborigines - ab o RIJ i neez
   C. absorb - ab ZORB
   D. acclimate - a KLI mat

2. A. accolade - ak o LAID   B. acetic - a SEE tik
   C. acumen - AK u men   D. adagion - a DAH jo

3. A. address - a DRESS   B. adobe - a DO be
   C. aegis - A jis   D. aesthete - ES theet

4. A. alias - A lee as   B. codicil - KOD i sil
   C. exit - IK sit   D. cache - CATCH

5. A. draught - DRAWT   B. drought - DROUT
   C. almond - AH mund   D. daub - DAWB

6. A. apiary - A pee er i   B. clique - KLIK
   C. circuitous - ser CUE i tus   D. crochet - kro SHAY

7. A. apparatus - ap a RAY tus   B. comptroller - kon TROL er
   C. apricot - A pri kot   D. coup - KOOP

8. A. coupe - koo PAY   B. coupon - CUE pon
   C. autopsy - AW top see   D. awry - a RYE

9. A. bailiwick - BALE i wik
   B. blackguard - BLAG ard
   C. dinghy - DIN jee
   D. cosmopolite - koz MOP o lite

10. A. auxiliary - awg ZIL ya ree
    B. bouquet - boo KAY
    C. brooch - BROCH
    D. chic - CHICK

KEY (CORRECT ANSWERS)

1. C
2. C
3. C
4. D
5. A

6. B
7. D
8. B
9. C
10. D

TEST 5

SPELLING

DIRECTIONS: One word in each lettered group is misspelled. Indicate the letter of the misspelled word.

1. A. abhorrent B. aquittal
   C. accessible D. ammeter   1.____

2. A. amanuensis B. annihalate
   C. battalion D. beneficent   2.____

3. A. cateclysm B. catechism
   C. beneficiary D. catarrh   3.____

4. A. avoirdupois B. catercornered
   C. cemetary D. caterpillar   4.____

5. A. cerement B. chalcedony
   C. effervesence D. collectible   5.____

6. A. chiffonier B. coalesce
   C. exorcise D. friccasee   6.____

7. A. consencus B. corollary
   C. denouement D. desuetude   7.____

8. A. dysentery B. emissary
   C. gazzetteer D. fuchsia   8.____

9. A. ecquinoctial B. evanescent
   C. excrescence D. exudation   9.____

10. A. Fahrenheit B. in as much as
    C. frontispiece D. imbroglio   10.____

11. A. gunwhale B. intercede
    C. irascible D. kaleidoscope   11.____

12. A. indefatigable B. supercede
    C. iridescence D. malleable   12.____

13. A. medallion B. moiety
    C. obsequies D. mayonaise   13.____

14. A. omniscience B. pavilion
    C. penitentiary D. pantomine   14.____

15. A. proscenium B. putrify
    C. ramify D. liquefy   15.____

16. A. predecessor B. plenipotentiary
    C. salutery D. solder   16.____

17. A. sasparilla B. stertorous
    C. supererogate D. vilify   17.____

18. A. soliloquy B. vicisitude 18._____
    C. somnambulance D. labyrinth

19. A. chrysalis B. corroborative 19._____
    C. Czechoslovakia D. Cincinati

20. A. idiocyncrasy B. crystallize 20._____
    C. deficiency D. dhoti

21. A. threshold B. withold 21._____
    C. newsstand D. peccadillo

22. A. prejudicial B. inoculate 22._____
    C. procedures D. inocuous

23. A. practitioner B. oriel 23._____
    C. ormulu D. resusitate

24. A. ricochet B. raillery 24._____
    C. garulous D. complaisant

25. A. predeliction B. sacrilegious 25._____
    C. antedate D. tourniquet

KEY (CORRECT ANSWERS)

1. B   11. A
2. B   12. B
3. A   13. D
4. C   14. D
5. C   15. B

6. D   16. C
7. A   17. A
8. C   18. B
9. A   19. D
10. B   20. A

21. B
22. D
23. D
24. C
25. A

TEST 6

SYLLABIFICATION

DIRECTIONS: In the following groups, only one word in each group is syllabificated correctly. Indicate the letter of the CORRECT syllabification.

1. A. ser vice a ble B. serv ice a ble 1.___
   C. serv i ce a ble D. ser vice able

2. A. ac ci den tal ly B. ace iden tal ly 2.___
   C. ac cid ent al ly D. ac ci dent al ly

3. A. grat u i tous B. grat ui tous 3.___
   C. gra tu i tous D. gratu i tous

4. A. mil len nium B. mill en ni um 4.___
   C. mil len ni um D. mill enn i um

5. A. o cca sion al ly B. oc ca sion al ly 5.___
   C. oc ca sio nal ly D. occa sion ally

6. A. opt im is tic B. op tim is tic 6.___
   C. opt i mis tic D. op ti mis tic

7. A. im me di ate ly B. im med i ate ly 7.___
   C. imm ed i ate ly D. im med iate ly

8. A. ca fe te ri a B. ca fet er i a 8.___
   C. caf e te ri a D. ca fe ter i a

9. A. lab o ra to ry B. la bo ra to ry 9.___
   C. lab o rat o ry D. la bor a to ry

10. A. pre pa ra tion B. prep ar a tion 10.___
    C. prep a ra tion D. pre par a tion

11. A. un an i mous B. u na ni mous 11.___
    C. unan i mous D. u nan i mous

12. A. pneum o ni a B. pneu mon i a 12.___
    C. pneu mo ni a D. pneu mo ni a

13. A. misc el lan e ous B. mis cel la ne ous 13.___
    C. mis cell a ne ous D. mis cel lan e ous

14. A. mul ti plic i ty B. mult i pli ci ty 14.___
    C. mul tip li ci ty D. mul tip lic i ty

15. A. part ic u lar B. par tic u lar 15.___
    C. part i cu lar D. par ti cu lar

KEY (CORRECT ANSWERS)

1. B
2. A
3. C
4. C
5. B

6. D
7. A
8. C
9. A
10. C

11. D
12. C
13. B
14. A
15. B

TEST 7

USAGE

DIRECTIONS: In each of the following groups of sentences, there are three sentences which are correct and one which is incorrect because it contains an error in grammar, usage, diction, or punctuation. Indicate the letter of the INCORRECT sentence.

1. A. I read political science books as a kind of duty, not for pleasure.
    B. You needn't go to all that expense for me.
    C. It will be extremely interesting to note the varied reactions of the other participants.
    D. Please do not be angry with me, because it really was not my fault.

2. A. We go there by boat and return by train.
    B. He wrote home for his bathing trunks, tennis racket, and set of golf clubs.
    C. Take me to his home, and I will tell him myself.
    D. The autobiography of George Bernard Shaw by Ernest Jones was assigned for reading by my English teacher.

3. A. Everyone was given his fair share.
    B. If the river will rise much higher, we may have a flood.
    C. There were, in the early years of this century, many more horses than automobiles.
    D. Either your enunciation is faulty or I am hard of hearing.

4. A. The boy assured his teacher that he would pass the tests with ease.
    B. Every person in these two buildings has to meet their responsibilities.
    C. Thunderstorms will invariably follow a lengthy hot spell.
    D. I believe the boy to be him.

5. A. I lay it on the bench before I left.
    B. She wrung the clothes before she bought a washing machine.
    C. We have drunk all the water.
    D. The wind has blown like this all night.

6. A. I like Shakespeare's HAMLET better than any of his plays.
    B. The roads are in poor condition because of the torrential rains.
    C. They robbed the child.
    D. They have stolen my cash.

7. A. If the winner *of* the contest were here, I would give him his medal.
    B. I hope my son graduates junior high school next June.
    C. Now is the time to make sure that we have beaten that team.
    D. We believe that those books are up to date.

8. A. Be careful that you do not slip on that oily surface.
    B. I hope to be able to take notes during his worth-while lecture.
    C. I think that phenomena is worth photographing.
    D. It occurred in the 1960's, not during the 1950's.

9. A. New York is larger than any city in Europe.
    B. Just as we reached the boat landing, the weather changed.
    C. Coming around the curve, the large house was seen.
    D. Generally speaking, my daughter is a good student.

10. A. Place the children's toys above the others.
    B. It was more unique that I thought it would be.
    C. It was my opinion, albeit an erroneous one, that he was the best swimmer on the team.
    D. The typewriter's ribbon was frayed.

11. A. The chances are that Ted's relatives believe in his honesty.
    B. I am glad that you think this was so.
    C. Give it to the club to which my grandmother belongs.
    D. I am in New York for ten years.

12. A. I have heard that he is never returning.
    B. In the last century it was especially fashionable to dress in that manner.
    C. This data, in my opinion, is incorrect.
    D. It is a highly selective procedure which must be followed.

13. A. She sat besides me on the couch.
    B. Billy is the best Spanish scholar of the three boys.
    C. It is gratifying to know that the city school system's strengths are being publicized.
    D. I do not have very much faith in his changing his mind.

14. A. I think that he should be feeling somewhat better.
    B. Do as she does if you want to do it correctly.
    C. I am surely glad that he was able to pass the test.
    D. Hide it some place.

15. A. He seemed to be possessed by an evil spirit.
    B. I think that his point of view is different from mine, but I still believe that I am correct.
    C. I agree to the new plan, but I disagree with him in regard to how it is to be accomplished.
    D. He has the natural desire to be independent from his parents.

16. A. Whenever she went to school she learned a lot.
    B. We had hoped to be on time, but we were late.
    C. My greatest fear, however, was overcome at the last moment.
    D. The two painters' works were displayed at the gallery.

17. A. The check from the Treasury Department will arrive on Monday, January 23.
    B. James was not sure that it was Jane and me at the party.
    C. I do not know if the search for William and her has been made.
    D. There were many accidents on the highway, but the toll was less than had been anticipated.

    17.____

18. A. A baby girl was just what we wanted.
    B. His vote was the larger of the two candidates.
    C. That boy had neither money or influence, and I do not know what chances of success he had.
    D. I may lie down on that bed if I get tired.

    18.____

19. A. He doesn't live too far from his friend's home.
    B. The northeast was covered with snow.
    C. Let's cut it into six portions so that we can each have a piece.
    D. The boy did six days' work.

    19.____

20. A. It was in first-class condition, and I decided to keep it.
    B. It was a highly polished piece of jewelry.
    C. The twins, not their little brother, has the measles.
    D. That is the most important document in the history of our country.

    20.____

KEY (CORRECT ANSWERS)

1.	A	11.	D
2.	D	12.	C
3.	B	13.	A
4.	B	14.	D
5.	A	15.	D
6.	A	16.	A
7.	B	17.	B
8.	C	18.	C
9.	C	19.	B
10.	B	20.	C

TEST 8

VOCABULARY

DIRECTIONS: Select the word or phrase NEAREST in meaning or MOST CLEARLY related to the word in capital letters.

1. CONCATENATION 1.____
    - A. chain
    - B. loud noise
    - C. convex
    - D. concentration

2. PALLIATE 2.____
    - A. touch
    - B. mitigate
    - C. club
    - D. osculate

3. MALINGERER 3.____
    - A. shirker
    - B. worker
    - C. artisan
    - D. artesian

4. SALIENT 4.____
    - A. salty
    - B. salaried
    - C. prominent
    - D. lucky

5. ANTECEDENT 5.____
    - A. preceding
    - B. occurring later
    - C. ancestor
    - D. relative

6. AMICABLE 6.____
    - A. enigmatic
    - B. hostile
    - C. ambient
    - D. friendly

7. PALPABLE 7.____
    - A. fluttering
    - B. reddish in color
    - C. tangible
    - D. helpless

8. IMMUTABLE 8.____
    - A. unclear
    - B. dull
    - C. precise
    - D. unchangeable

9. DESULTORY 9.____
    - A. aimless
    - B. purposeful
    - C. dismal
    - D. desolate

10. NEBULOUS 10.____
    - A. untidy
    - B. clear
    - C. vague
    - D. strong

11. SAGACIOUS 11.____
    - A. sagging
    - B. sturdy
    - C. containing herbs
    - D. discerning

12. FRENETIC 12.____
    - A. frantic
    - B. quiet
    - C. early
    - D. bumpy

13. TURBID   13.____
    A. numb   B. swollen   C. cloudy   D. unwieldy

14. DECENNIAL   14.____
    A. happening every 10 years
    B. of a generation
    C. occurring irregularly
    D. celebration

15. MORIBUND   15.____
    A. sarcastic   B. zealous
    C. analagous   D. near death

16. ABYSS   16.____
    A. immeasurable space   B. abutment
    C. prioress   D. lake

17. LANGUID   17.____
    A. horizontal   B. strong
    C. energetic   D. weak

18. DEBILITY   18.____
    A. diabolical   B. indebtedness
    C. an accounting term   D. infirmity

19. AVUNCULAR   19.____
    A. European railroad   B. like an uncle
    C. shevel   D. unfriendly

20. LITTORAL   20.____
    A. a coastal region   B. true
    C. undeviating   D. literary

21. SANGUINE   21.____
    A. grotesque   B. partial
    C. hopeless   D. hopeful

22. SAPIENT   22.____
    A. foolish   B. ill-informed
    C. wise   D. insipid

23. TAUTOLOGY   23.____
    A. needless repetition   B. gesticulation
    C. tension   D. education

24. QUONDAM   24.____
    A. member of nobility   B. former
    C. certain   D. lady-in-waiting

25. JEJUNE
    A. jellylike
    B. gentle
    C. lacking nourishing quality
    D. graceful

26. EPITAPH
    A. curse
    B. illness
    C. skin
    D. inscription on a tomb

27. NADIR
    A. negative answer
    B. culmination
    C. lowest point
    D. zenith

28. BADINAGE
    A. banter
    B. binding for a wound
    C. evil
    D. cavil

29. CYGNET
    A. ring
    B. a young swan
    C. signature
    D. token

30. PECULATE
    A. gamble
    B. imitate
    C. steal public money
    D. interrogate

31. PROFLIGATE
    A. make a profit
    B. church official
    C. soothsayer
    D. dissolute

32. PROLIX
    A. close   B. promise   C. verbose   D. profit

33. PRETERNATURAL
    A. strange
    B. distant
    C. unapproachable
    D. dusty

34. CONCENTRIC
    A. having a common center
    B. growing a hundred feet apart
    C. central
    D. oval

35. SYCOPHANT
    A. flatterer   B. invalid   C. relative   D. enemy

36. UNCTUOUS

    A. oily
    B. pleasant
    C. progressive
    D. tyrannical

37. UBIQUITOUS

    A. vicious
    B. large
    C. grotesque
    D. omnipresent

38. INELUCTABLE

    A. dark
    B. illuminated
    C. inevitable
    D. unclear

39. VIABLE

    A. capable of living
    B. visible
    C. conquering
    D. edible

40. LEXICON

    A. tax booklet
    B. almanac
    C. dictionary
    D. bulletin

41. SENTENTIOUS

    A. sentimental
    B. coarse
    C. terse
    D. up to date

42. VERACIOUS

    A. hungry
    B. truthful
    C. pertinent
    D. referring to spring

43. NOISOME

    A. loud
    B. inquisitive
    C. temporary
    D. harmful

44. COZEN

    A. match
    B. relative
    C. mark
    D. cheat

45. DILATORY

    A. restless
    B. rebellious
    C. derogatory
    D. tending to delay

46. CIRRUS

    A. robust
    B. diligent
    C. cloud
    D. precise

47. CONTUMACY

    A. defiance of authority
    B. agreement of friends
    C. disappointment
    D. connection

48. INCIPIENCE

    A. ending
    B. beginning
    C. foolishness
    D. growth

49. IRREPARABLE

   A. temporary
   C. intestate
   B. oscillating
   D. irremediable

49.____

50. EXPOSTULATE

   A. shatter
   C. remonstrate
   B. exonerate
   D. vanquish

50.____

KEY (CORRECT ANSWERS)

1. A	11. D	21. D	31. D	41. C
2. B	12. A	22. C	32. C	42. B
3. A	13. C	23. A	33. A	43. D
4. C	14. A	24. B	34. A	44. D
5. A	15. D	25. C	35. A	45. D
6. D	16. A	26. D	36. A	46. C
7. C	17. D	27. C	37. D	47. A
8. D	18. D	28. A	38. C	48. B
9. A	19. B	29. B	39. A	49. D
10. C	20. A	30. C	40. C	50. C

SPELLING

COMMENTARY

Spelling forms an integral part of tests of academic aptitude and achievement and of general and mental ability. Moreover, the spelling question is a staple of verbal and clerical tests in civil service entrance and promotional examinations.

Perhaps, the most rewarding way to learn to spell successfully is the direct, functional approach of learning to spell correctly, both orally and in writing, all words as they appear, both singly and in context.

In accordance with this positive method, the spelling question is presented here in "test" form, as it might appear on an actual examination.

The spelling question may appear on examinations in the following format:
> Four words are listed in each question. These are lettered A, B, C, and D. A fifth option, E, is also given, which always reads "none misspelled." The examinee is to select one of the five (lettered) choices: either A, B, C, or D if one of the words is misspelled, or item E, none misspelled, if all four words have been correctly spelled in the question.

SAMPLE QUESTIONS

The directions for this part are approximately as follows:

DIRECTIONS: Mark the space corresponding to the one MISSPELLED word in each of the following groups of words. If NO word is misspelled, mark the last space on the answer sheet.

SAMPLE O
- A. walk
- B. talk
- C. play
- D. dance
- E. *none misspelled*

Since none of the words is misspelled, E would be marked on the answer sheet.

SAMPLE OO
- A. seize
- B. yield
- C. define
- D. reccless
- E. *none misspelled*

Since "reccless" (correct spelling, reckless) has been misspelled, D would be marked on the answer. sheet

SPELLING

SAMPLE QUESTION

DIRECTIONS: The spelling test is designed to resemble a proofreading task. You are presented with a passage. Each line of the passage is considered one test question. You are to read the passage and indicate how many spelling errors are contained in each line. In some cases, a spelling error will consist of the use of the wrong form of a word that has several correct spellings. The different correct spellings of such words have different meanings, for example "to," "two," and "too." Be sure that you look for these kinds of errors. *PRINT THE LETTER OF THE CORRECT ANSWER IN THE SPACE AT THE RIGHT.*

KEY

A = The line contains no spelling errors.
B = There is one (1) spelling error in the line.
C = There are two (2) spelling errors in the line.
D = There are three (3) or more spelling errors in the line.

1. The main reasons for in-service training are to inprove the work being done by

2. employees in there present jobs and to meet the system and program goals of the

3. agency. It is the responsablity of managers to suport and encourage teh use of

4. skills learned in training classes. In-service training will be done during normal work

5. hours and will be paied for by the employer.

KEY (CORRECT ANSWERS)

1. The correct answer is B. There is one spelling error. The word "improve" is misspelled as "inprove".

2. The correct answer is B. The word "there" is not spelled correctly for the use of the word in this sentence. In this case, we need the plural, possessive pronoun "their", so one spelling error is found in this line.

3. The correct answer is D. There are three misspelled words in this line: "responsibility," "support," and "the".

4. The correct answer is A. This line contains no spelling errors.

5. The correct answer is B. This line contains one spelling error. The word "paied" is misspelled and should be "paid" or "payed". Both are acceptable forms though "paid" is probably more commonly used.

TESTS IN SPELLING

EXAMINATION SECTION
TEST 1

DIRECTIONS: In each question of the following tests, select the letter of the one MIS-SPELLED word in each of the listed groups of five (5) words. *PRINT THE LETTER OF THE CORRECT ANSWER IN THE SPACE AT THE RIGHT.*

1.	A.	break	B.	scenary	C.	business	D.	arouse	E.	religious	1.____
2.	A.	rinsed	B.	height	C.	jewel	D.	furtile	E.	doesn't	2.____
3.	A.	perform	B.	divide	C.	apologize	D.	occasion	E.	acheive	3.____
4.	A.	asending	B.	benefit	C.	disappear	D.	operate	E.	grammar	4.____
5.	A.	forty	B.	precede	C.	annuel	D.	parable	E.	curiosity	5.____
6.	A.	irritable	B.	stupefy	C.	gaseous	D.	millionair	E.	luscious	6.____
7.	A.	invincible	B.	Slav	C.	supersede	D.	haddock	E.	fatigueing	7.____
8.	A.	scissors	B.	explanatory	C.	bituminus	D.	heifer	E.	cessation	8.____
9.	A.	caramel	B.	Wisconsin	C.	acquarium	D.	sterilize	E.	pseudonym	9.____
10.	A.	precipise	B.	knapsack	C.	brilliance	D.	challenge	E.	decrepit	10.____
11.	A.	certificate	B.	ajourn	C.	apparel	D.	aggression	E.	symphony	11.____
12.	A.	Norwegian	B.	constent	C.	interruption	D.	wouldn't	E.	article	12.____
13.	A.	heros	B.	logical	C.	guarantee	D.	imprison	E.	legitimate	13.____
14.	A.	happiness	B.	weird	C.	miscellaneous	D.	village	E.	arguement	14.____
15.	A.	wretched	B.	tendency	C.	controversiel	D.	arbitrary	E.	denial	15.____
16.	A.	lonliness	B.	safeguard	C.	pilot	D.	chiefs	E.	obstacle	16.____
17.	A.	shining	B.	professional	C.	scheme	D.	excitment	E.	expectancy	17.____
18.	A.	negative	B.	editorial	C.	clothe	D.	economize	E.	suprising	18.____
19.	A.	illegal	B.	opinion	C.	discription	D.	rationalize	E.	picnicking	19.____
20.	A.	circuit	B.	sponser	C.	exasperate	D.	volume	E.	valuable	20.____

KEY (CORRECT ANSWERS)

1. B. scenery
2. D. fertile
3. E. achieve
4. A. ascending
5. C. annual
6. D. millionaire
7. E. fatiguing
8. C. bituminous
9. C. aquarium
10. A. precipice
11. B. adjourn
12. B. constant
13. A. heroes
14. E. argument
15. C. controversial
16. A. loneliness
17. D. excitement
18. E. surprising
19. C. description
20. B. sponsor

TEST 2

DIRECTIONS: In each question of the following tests, select the letter of the one MIS-SPELLED word in each of the listed groups of five (5) words. *PRINT THE LETTER OF THE CORRECT ANSWER IN THE SPACE AT THE RIGHT.*

1. A. procession B. performance C. poize D. allied E. discipline 1.____
2. A. advocate B. saleries C. commercial D. expense E. forcibly 2.____
3. A. enormous B. enterprise C. florist D. humilliate E. careful 3.____
4. A. treachery B. bolstor C. simplify D. revelation E. reciprocal 4.____
5. A. witness B. derisive C. typewriter D. relative E. medecine 5.____
6. A. betrayel B. forsaken C. impetuous D. finesse E. recognize 6.____
7. A. forcast B. pastime C. several D. ridiculous E. cleanliness 7.____
8. A. correspond B. conceited C. implies D. receptacle E. amatuer 8.____
9. A. captain B. definitely C. credited D. cordially E. couragous 9.____
10. A. parallel B. various C. obnoxious D. assurence E. grateful 10.____
11. A. feirce B. ascent C. allies D. doctor E. coming 11.____
12. A. hopeless B. absense C. foretell D. certain E. similar 12.____
13. A. advise B. muscle C. manual D. provocation E. copywright 13.____
14. A. behooves B. reservoir C. frostbiten D. squalor E. ambuscade 14.____
15. A. systematic B. precious C. tremenduous D. insulation E. brilliant 15.____
16. A. significant B. jurisdiction C. libel D. monkies E. legacy 16.____
17. A. delicatessen B. occupansy C. gorgeous D. consolation E. anxiety 17.____
18. A. tyranny B. perennial C. catagory D. inspector E. confidential 18.____
19. A. symbol B. formerly C. warring D. caution E. bankrupcy 19.____
20. A. aperture B. cellaphane C. diagnosis D. intestinal E. mahogany 20.____

KEY (CORRECT ANSWERS)

1. C. poise
2. B. salaries
3. D. humiliate
4. B. bolster
5. E. medicine
6. A. betrayal
7. A. forecast
8. E. amateur
9. E. courageous
10. D. assurance
11. A. fierce
12. B. absence
13. E. copyright
14. C. frostbitten
15. C. tremendous
16. D. monkeys
17. B. occupancy
18. C. category
19. E. bankruptcy
20. B. cellophane

TEST 3

DIRECTIONS: In each question of the following tests, select the letter of the one MISSPELLED word in each of the listed groups of five (5) words. *PRINT THE LETTER OF THE CORRECT ANSWER IN THE SPACE AT THE RIGHT.*

1. A. pitiful B. latter C. ommitted D. agreement E. reconcile 1._____
2. A. banaana B. routine C. likewise D. indecent E. habitually 2._____
3. A. relieve B. copys C. ninety D. crowded E. electoral 3._____
4. A. adviseable B. illustrative C. financial D. nevertheless E. chimneys 4._____
5. A. prisioner B. immediate C. statistics D. surgeon E. treachery 5._____
6. A. option B. extradite C. comparitive D. jealousy E. illusion 6._____
7. A. handicaped B. assurance C. sympathy D. speech E. dining 7._____
8. A. recommend B. carraige C. disapprove D. independent E. mortgage 8._____
9. A. systematic B. ingenuity C. tenet D. uncanny E. intrigueing 9._____
10. A. arduous B. hideous C. fervant D. companies E. breach 10._____
11. A. together B. attempt C. loyality D. innocent E. rinse 11._____
12. A. argueing B. emergency C. kindergarten D. religious E. schedule 12._____
13. A. society B. anticipate C. dissatisfy D. responsable E. temporary 13._____
14. A. chaufeur B. grammar C. planned D. dining room E. accurate 14._____
15. A. confidence B. maturity C. aspiration D. evasion E. insurence 15._____
16. A. unnecessary B. dirigible C. transparant D. similar E. appetite 16._____
17. A. regional B. slimy C. tumbler D. educator E. femenine 17._____
18. A. orchestration B. proclamation C. pretext D. rearmement E. invoice 18._____
19. A. fragrant B. independent C. halves D. parallel E. advantagous 19._____
20. A. championing B. conversion C. predominent D. puppet E. anarchist 20._____

87

KEY (CORRECT ANSWERS)

1. C. omitted
2. A. banana
3. B. copies
4. A. advisable
5. A. prisoner
6. C. comparative
7. A. handicapped
8. B. carriage
9. E. intriguing
10. C. fervent
11. C. loyalty
12. A. arguing
13. D. responsible
14. A. chauffeur
15. E. insurance
16. C. transparent
17. E. feminine
18. D. rearmament
19. E. advantageous
20. C. predominant

TEST 4

DIRECTIONS: In each question of the following tests, select the letter of the one MISSPELLED word in each of the listed groups of five (5) words. *PRINT THE LETTER OF THE CORRECT ANSWER IN THE SPACE AT THE RIGHT.*

1. A. wrist B. welfare C. necessity D. scenery E. tendancy 1.____
2. A. commiting B. accusation C. endurance D. agreeable E. excitable 2.____
3. A. despair B. surgury C. privilege D. appreciation E. journeying 3.____
4. A. cameos B. propaganda C. delicious D. heathen E. interupt 4.____
5. A. relieve B. disappear C. development D. matress E. ninety-nine 5.____
6. A. finally B. bulitin C. doctor D. desirable E. sincerely 6.____
7. A. wrest B. array C. auspices D. sacrafice E. generations 7.____
8. A. liquid B. vegetable C. silence D. familiar E. fasinate 8.____
9. A. tomato B. suspence C. leisure D. license E. permanent 9.____
10. A. characteristic B. soliciting C. repititious D. immediately E. extravagant 10.____
11. A. travel B. conductor C. equiping D. proposal E. twofold 11.____
12. A. philosopher B. minority C. managment D. emergency E. bibliography 12.____
13. A. constructive B. employee C. stalwart D. masterpeice E. theoretical 13.____
14. A. dissappoint B. volcanic C. illiterate D. myth E. superficial 14.____
15. A. totally B. penninsula C. sandwich D. ripening E. salvation 15.____
16. A. pastel B. aisle C. primarly D. journalistic E. diminished 16.____
17. A. warrier B. unification C. enamel D. defendant E. sustained 17.____
18. A. incidental B. lubricent C. conversion D. jurisdiction E. interpretation 18.____
19. A. auxilary B. boundaries C. session D. fabric E. ceiling 19.____
20. A. imperious B. depreciate C. rebutal D. wharf E. giddy 20.____

KEY (CORRECT ANSWERS)

1. E. tendency
2. A. committing
3. B. surgery
4. E. interrupt
5. D. mattress
6. B. bulletin
7. D. sacrifice
8. E. fascinate
9. B. suspense
10. C. repetitious
11. C. equipping
12. C. management
13. D. masterpiece
14. A. disappoint
15. B. peninsula
16. C. primarily
17. A. warrior
18. B. lubricant
19. A. auxiliary
20. C. rebuttal

TEST 5

DIRECTIONS: In each question of the following tests, select the letter of the one MIS-SPELLED word in each of the listed groups of five (5) words. *PRINT THE LETTER OF THE CORRECT ANSWER IN THE SPACE AT THE RIGHT.*

1. A. renewel B. charitable C. abrupt D. humankind E. strengthen 1.____
2. A. khaki B. survival C. laboratory D. intensefied E. stature 2.____
3. A. diesel B. cocoa C. alphabettical D. visible E. overlaid 3.____
4. A. neutral B. ballot C. parallysis D. enterprise E. abnormal 4.____
5. A. ironical B. mountainous C. permissible D. carburetor E. blizard 5.____
6. A. penalty B. affidavit C. document D. notery E. valid 6.____
7. A. provocative B. apparition C. forfiet D. procedure E. requisite 7.____
8. A. terrifying B. museum C. minimum D. competitors E. efficiensy 8.____
9. A. hangar B. spokesman C. mustache D. cathederal E. pumpkin 9.____
10. A. guidance B. until C. usage D. loyalist E. prarie 10.____
11. A. obnoxious B. balancing C. squadron D. illicit E. clearence 11.____
12. A. timetable B. gymnasium C. humid D. disolve E. gracious 12.____
13. A. spiciness B. biblography C. injunction D. mediator E. discriminate 13.____
14. A. endearing B. mannerism C. predecesser D. gardener E. instantaneous 14.____
15. A. shrewdness B. purified C. acceptable D. uniqueness E. corugated 15.____
16. A. baptize B. diversity C. parochial D. abandonning E. hypnosis 16.____
17. A. deteryorate B. priority C. cuddle D. shrivel E. narcotic 17.____
18. A. neutrality B. horseradish C. contemporaries D. inducement E. prelimnery 18.____
19. A. eventually B. disilusioned C. divine D. inimitable E. fraudulent 19.____
20. A. verticle B. musician C. tomatoes D. athletic E. decision 20.____

KEY (CORRECT ANSWERS)

1. A. renewal
2. D. intensified
3. C. alphabetical
4. C. paralysis
5. E. blizzard
6. D. notary
7. C. forfeit
8. E. efficiency
9. D. cathedral
10. E. prairie
11. E. clearance
12. D. dissolve
13. B. bibliography
14. C. predecessor
15. E. corrugated
16. D. abandoning
17. A. deteriorate
18. E. preliminary
19. B. disillusioned
20. A. vertical

TEST 6

DIRECTIONS: In each question of the following tests, select the letter of the one MISSPELLED word in each of the listed groups of five (5) words. *PRINT THE LETTER OF THE CORRECT ANSWER IN THE SPACE AT THE RIGHT.*

1. A. advising B. recognize C. seize D. supply E. tradegy 1.____
2. A. intensive B. stationary C. benifit D. equipped E. preferring 2.____
3. A. predjudice B. pervade C. excel D. capitol E. chimneys 3.____
4. A. all right B. ninty C. cronies D. nervous E. separate 4.____
5. A. atheletic B. queue C. furl D. schedule E. abusing 5.____
6. A. skein B. wholesome C. witches D. coherent E. defenite 6.____
7. A. aggravate B. counsel C. deplorable D. proficency E. catarrh 7.____
8. A. suppressed B. lugubrious C. pecuniary D. boulevard E. fourty-fourth 8.____
9. A. militarism B. pilot C. crimnal D. monotonous E. tendency 9.____
10. A. prevalent B. berth C. auxiliary D. privileges E. women's 10.____
11. A. incurred B. cieling C. strengthen D. carnage E. typical 11.____
12. A. twins B. year's C. acutely D. changible E. facility 12.____
13. A. deliscious B. enormous C. likeness D. witnesses E. commodity 13.____
14. A. scenes B. enlargement C. discretion D. acknowledging E. sesion 14.____
15. A. annum B. strenuous C. tretchery D. infamy E. opporture 15.____
16. A. marmelade B. loot C. kinsman D. crochet E. hawser 16.____
17. A. fireman B. glossary C. tuition D. dissapoint E. refrigerator 17.____
18. A. inadequate B. municpal C. bored D. masonic E. utilize 18.____
19. A. partisan B. temporary C. cawleflower D. obstinacy E. hyperbole 19.____
20. A. people's B. spherical C. foliage D. everlasting E. feesable 20.____

KEY (CORRECT ANSWERS)

1. E. tragedy
2. C. benefit
3. A. prejudice
4. B. ninety
5. A. athletic
6. E. definite
7. D. proficiency
8. E. forty-fourth
9. C. criminal
10. D. privileges
11. B. ceiling
12. D. changeable
13. A. delicious
14. E. session
15. C. treachery
16. A. marmalade
17. D. disappoint
18. B. municipal
19. C. cauliflower
20. E. feasible

TEST 7

DIRECTIONS: In each question of the following tests, select the letter of the one MISSPELLED word in each of the listed groups of five (5) words. *PRINT THE LETTER OF THE CORRECT ANSWER IN THE SPACE AT THE RIGHT.*

1. A. inferred B. whisle C. jovial D. conscript E. gracious 1.____
2. A. tantalizing B. ominous C. conductor D. duchess E. telegram 2.____
3. A. reconcile B. primitive C. sausy D. quinine E. cede 3.____
4. A. immagine B. viaduct C. chisel D. Saturn E. currant 4.____
5. A. amplify B. greace C. cholera D. perilous E. theology 5.____
6. A. pursevere B. deodorize C. ligament D. illuminate E. dropsy 6.____
7. A. legible B. frivolously C. precious D. rezemblence E. congeal 7.____
8. A. intramural B. epidemic C. germicide D. anonymous E. acurracy 8.____
9. A. affable B. hazard C. combustable D. lacquer E. stationary 9.____
10. A. sagacious B. interpreter C. poultise D. dinosaur E. dismal 10.____
11. A. acknowledging B. deligate C. foliage D. staid E. loot 11.____
12. A. gardian B. losing C. notwithstanding D. worlds E. typhoid 12.____
13. A. medal B. utilize C. efficiency D. apricot E. soliceting 13.____
14. A. museum B. Christian C. possesion D. occasional E. bored 14.____
15. A. capitol B. sieze C. premises D. fragrance E. tonnage 15.____
16. A. requisition B. faculties C. canon D. chaufur E. stomach 16.____
17. A. solemn B. ascertain C. I'll D. chef E. delinquant 17.____
18. A. parliments B. distributor C. voluntary D. lovable E. counsel 18.____
19. A. morale B. democrat C. rhumatism D. dormitory E. leased 19.____
20. A. screech B. missapropriating C. courtesies D. wretched E. furlough 20.____

KEY (CORRECT ANSWERS)

1. B. whistle
2. E. telegram
3. C. saucy
4. A. imagine
5. B. grease
6. A. persevere
7. D. resemblance
8. E. accuracy
9. C. combustible
10. C. poultice
11. B. delegate
12. A. guardian
13. E. soliciting
14. C. possession
15. B. seize
16. D. chauffeur
17. E. delinquent
18. A. parliaments
19. C. rheumatism
20. B. misappropriating

TEST 8

DIRECTIONS: In each question of the following tests, select the letter of the one MIS-SPELLED word in each of the listed groups of five (5) words. *PRINT THE LETTER OF THE CORRECT ANSWER IN THE SPACE AT THE RIGHT.*

1. A. typhoid B. tarriff C. visible D. accent E. countries 1.____
2. A. dizzy B. leggings C. steak D. compaine E. interior 2.____
3. A. profit B. tiranny C. shocked D. response E. innocent 3.____
4. A. freshman B. vague C. larsiny D. ignorant E. worrying 4.____
5. A. disatesfied B. jealous C. unfortunately D. economical E. lettuce 5.____
6. A. based B. primarily C. condemned D. accompanied E. dupped 6.____
7. A. superntendant B. veil C. congenial D. quantities E. ere 7.____
8. A. unanimous B. dessert C. undoubtedly D. kolera E. nuisance 8.____
9. A. woman's B. bulletin C. 'tis D. Pullman E. envellop 9.____
10. A. initiate B. guardian C. pagent D. wretched E. adieu 10.____
11. A. continually B. guild C. vegtable D. vague E. patience 11.____
12. A. desease B. parole C. gallery D. awkward E. you'd 12.____
13. A. border B. warrant C. operated D. economics E. ilegal 13.____
14. A. fatal B. agatation C. obliged D. studying E. resignation 14.____
15. A. ammendment B. promptness C. glimpse D. canon E. tract 15.____
16. A. wholly B. apricot C. destruction D. pappal E. leisure 16.____
17. A. issuing B. rabbid C. unauthorized D. parasite E. khaki 17.____
18. A. nowadays B. courtesies C. negotiate D. gaurdian E. derrick 18.____
19. A. partisan B. seanse C. vacancy D. fragrance E. corps 19.____
20. A. equipped B. nuisance C. phrenoligist D. foreign E. insignia 20.____

KEY (CORRECT ANSWERS)

1. B. tariff
2. D. company
3. B. tyranny
4. C. larceny
5. A. dissatisfied
6. E. duped
7. A. superintendent
8. D. cholera
9. E. envelope
10. C. pageant
11. C. vegetable
12. A. disease
13. E. illegal
14. B. agitation
15. A. amendment
16. D. papal
17. B. rabid
18. D. guardian
19. B. seance
20. C. phrenologist

TEST 9

DIRECTIONS: In each question of the following tests, select the letter of the one MISSPELLED word in each of the listed groups of five (5) words. *PRINT THE LETTER OF THE CORRECT ANSWER IN THE SPACE AT THE RIGHT.*

1. A. frightfully B. mantain C. post office D. specific E. bachelor 1.____
2. A. cease B. turkeys C. woman's D. hustling E. weild 2.____
3. A. expedition B. valuoble C. typhoid D. grapevines E. advice 3.____
4. A. echoes B. absolutly C. foggy D. wretched E. Sabbath 4.____
5. A. screech B. motorist C. congresionel D. utilize E. eligible 5.____
6. A. quizzes B. coarse C. aquaintence D. exhibition E. totally 6.____
7. A. principle B. transferring C. statutes D. here's E. sergeon 7.____
8. A. porcilane B. primeval C. suite D. unauthorized E. declension 8.____
9. A. commodity B. mischevious C. galvanized D. ordinance E. tuition 9.____
10. A. Christian B. fraternity C. accompanying D. disernable E. inadequate 10.____
11. A. subsidy B. inference C. chronicle D. purchace E. adroit 11.____
12. A. resources B. cargoes C. oponent D. disbelief E. treasurer 12.____
13. A. origional B. provincial C. knuckle D. ridiculous E. ecstasy 13.____
14. A. attitude B. soloes C. occurred D. policies E. technique 14.____
15. A. opinionated B. quantity C. systematic D. drought E. confidencial 15.____
16. A. interim B. idleness C. accesion D. elite E. fungi 16.____
17. A. inarticulate B. servitude C. ejaculate D. herewith E. preceedence 17.____
18. A. experimental B. minority C. cultural D. expedient E. penant 18.____
19. A. apparently B. criticism C. justification D. physican E. simultaneous 19.____
20. A. accidentally B. overule C. unintentional D. talented E. maturation 20.____

KEY (CORRECT ANSWERS)

1. B. maintain
2. E. wield
3. B. valuable
4. B. absolutely
5. C. congressional
6. C. acquaintance
7. E. surgeon
8. A. porcelain
9. B. mischievous
10. D. discernible
11. D. purchase
12. C. opponent
13. A. original
14. B. solos
15. E. confidential
16. C. accession
17. E. precedence
18. E. pennant
19. D. physician
20. B. overrule

TEST 10

DIRECTIONS: In each question of the following tests, select the letter of the one MISSPELLED word in each of the listed groups of five (5) words. *PRINT THE LETTER OF THE CORRECT ANSWER IN THE SPACE AT THE RIGHT.*

1. A. liabillity   B. capacity   C. guidance   D. illegible   E. expedient   1.____
2. A. debris   B. apetite   C. mosquitoes   D. vessal   E. yacht   2.____
3. A. tireless   B. feindish   C. recruit   D. swarthy   E. sandal   3.____
4. A. redouble   B. wizard   C. murderer   D. hindrance   E. syncope   4.____
5. A. equalize   B. turbulent   C. repetitive   D. corronation   E. statistical   5.____
6. A. remittance   B. sensitivity   C. fatality   D. soprano   E. inconveniance   6.____
7. A. fraternity   B. plebeian   C. inteligible   D. trickster   E. expeditionary   7.____
8. A. gasous   B. consistency   C. brooches   D. magistrate   E. translucent   8.____
9. A. lightning   B. persistent   C. cynical   D. musician   E. recipricate   9.____
10. A. commodity   B. fictitous   C. rabid   D. gaiety   E. couldn't   10.____
11. A. visible   B. creditor   C. paradice   D. infinite   E. questionnaire   11.____
12. A. existence   B. disarming   C. endorsement   D. commercal   E. trigger   12.____
13. A. aluminum   B. stuning   C. allowance   D. irate   E. pleasantry   13.____
14. A. cipher   B. colloquial   C. envoy   D. pursued   E. writting   14.____
15. A. insurable   B. benign   C. influentual   D. sophomore   E. casualty   15.____
16. A. presentiment   B. theological   C. anatamy   D. eccentricity   E. amphibious   16.____
17. A. embargo   B. vocalize   C. recommend   D. confering   E. remunerate   17.____
18. A. tangent   B. fickel   C. circuit   D. mathematics   E. vegetarian   18.____
19. A. unscheduled   B. declension   C. secretariat   D. forsight   E. enamel   19.____
20. A. hygienic   B. arrogant   C. disbanded   D. census   E. memorandem   20.____

KEY (CORRECT ANSWERS)

1. A. liability
2. B. appetite
3. B. fiendish
4. C. murderer
5. D. coronation
6. E. inconvenience
7. C. intelligible
8. A. gaseous
9. E. reciprocate
10. B. fictitious
11. C. paradise
12. D. commercial
13. B. stunning
14. E. writing
15. C. influential
16. C. anatomy
17. D. conferring
18. B. fickle
19. D. foresight
20. E. memorandum

TESTS IN SPELLING

EXAMINATION SECTION
TEST 1

DIRECTIONS: In each question of the following tests, select the letter of the one MISSPELLED word in each of the listed groups of five (5) words. *PRINT THE LETTER OF THE CORRECT ANSWER IN THE SPACE AT THE RIGHT.*

1. A. barely   B. assigned   C. mechanical   D. concequently   E. lovingly   1.____
2. A. obedient   B. elaborate   C. disgust   D. bearing   E. ambasador   2.____
3. A. awkward   B. charitable   C. typhoid   D. compitition   E. ruffle   3.____
4. A. concervatory B. ninth   C. morsel   D. squirrels   E. luxury   4.____
5. A. loyalty   B. occasional   C. hosiery   D. bungalow   E. undicided   5.____
6. A. efficient B. suberb   C. achievement D. bored   E. specimen   6.____
7. A. adaquate   B. salaries   C. utilize   D. alcohol   E. colonel   7.____
8. A. forcibly   B. guardian   C. preceeding   D. quartile   E. quizzes   8.____
9. A. seiges   B. unanimous   C. ridiculous   D. everlasting   E. omissions   9.____
10. A. itemized B. ignoramus   C. adige   D. adieu   E. nickel   10.____
11. A. resources B. fileal   C. nervous   D. logical   E. certificate 11.____
12. A. wiring   B. turkeys   C. morass   D. obvious   E. bigimmy   12.____
13. A. affirmitive B. noisy   C. clothe   D. carnage   E. perceive   13.____
14. A. ignorant B. literally   C. humerists   D. business   E. awkward   14.____
15. A. thermometer B. tragady   C. partisan   D. kinsman   E. grandiose   15.____
16. A. fundamental B. herald   C. delinquent   D. kindergarden   E. ascertain   16.____
17. A. apropriation B. year's   C. vacancy   D. enthusiastic   E. dormitory   17.____
18. A. crochet   B. courtesies   C. troup   D. occasionally   E. spirits   18.____
19. A. typewriting B. inadequate C. legitimate   D. fuelless   E. restarant   19.____
20. A. tabloux   B. cooperage   C. wrapped   D. tenant   E. referring   20.____

KEY (CORRECT ANSWERS)

1. D. consequently
2. E. ambassador
3. D. competition
4. A. conservatory
5. E. undecided
6. B. suburb
7. A. adequate
8. C. preceding OR proceeding
9. A. sieges
10. C. adage
11. B. filial
12. E. bigamy
13. A. affirmative
14. C. humorists
15. B. tragedy
16. D. kindergarten
17. A. appropriation
18. C. troop OR troupe
19. E. restaurant
20. A. tableaux OR tableaus

TEST 2

DIRECTIONS: In each question of the following tests, select the letter of the one MISSPELLED word in each of the listed groups of five (5) words. *PRINT THE LETTER OF THE CORRECT ANSWER IN THE SPACE AT THE RIGHT.*

1. A. loot B. surgery C. breif D. talcum E. Christmas 1.____
2. A. commenced B. congenial C. fatal D. politician E. standerd 2.____
3. A. unbarable B. physician C. potato D. wiring E. adorable 3.____
4. A. error B. regretted C. instetute D. typhoid E. we're 4.____
5. A. merly B. opportunity C. patterns D. unctious E. righteous 5.____
6. A. luxury B. forty C. control D. originally E. intemate 6.____
7. A. plague B. ignorance C. poltrey D. hence E. bruise 7.____
8. A. athletic B. exebition C. leased D. interrupt E. spirits 8.____
9. A. destruction B. prairie C. quartet D. status E. competators 9.____
10. A. triumph B. utility C. loyalty D. antisapte E. crochet 10.____
11. A. lieutenant B. recrute C. thermometer D. quantities E. usefulness 11.____
12. A. wholly B. sitting C. probably D. criticism E. lynche 12.____
13. A. anteque B. galvanized C. mercantile D. academy E. defense 13.____
14. A. kinsman B. declaration C. absurd D. dispach E. patience 14.____
15. A. opportune B. abbuting C. warranted D. refrigerator E. raisin 15.____
16. A. deffered B. principalship C. lovable D. athletic E. conveniently 16.____
17. A. mislaid B. receipted C. skedule D. mission E. whereabouts 17.____
18. A. tuition B. unnatural C. remodel D. consequence E. misdameanor 18.____
19. A. assessment B. advises C. embassys D. border E. leased 19.____
20. A. morale B. legitemate C. infamy D. indebtedness E. technical 20.____

KEY (CORRECT ANSWERS)

1. C. brief
2. E. standard
3. A. unbearable
4. C. institute
5. A. merely
6. E. intimate
7. C. poultry OR paltry
8. B. exhibition
9. E. competition
10. D. anticipate
11. B. recruit
12. E. lynch
13. A. antique
14. D. dispatch
15. B. abutting
16. A. deferred OR differed
17. C. schedule
18. E. misdemeanor
19. C. embassies
20. B. legitimate

TEST 3

DIRECTIONS: In each question of the following tests, select the letter of the one MISSPELLED word in each of the listed groups of five (5) words. *PRINT THE LETTER OF THE CORRECT ANSWER IN THE SPACE AT THE RIGHT.*

1. A. stepfather B. fireman C. loot D. conclusivly E. commodity 1.____
2. A. mislaid B. roommate C. religous D. thesis E. temporary 2.____
3. A. statutes B. malice C. unbridled D. aisle E. cavelry 3.____
4. A. aknowledge B. immensely C. quantities D. erratic E. postponed 4.____
5. A. people's B. foreign C. obsticles D. opportunity E. cordially 5.____
6. A. fragrance B. burgaleries C. clothe D. twins E. herculean 6.____
7. A. warranted B. yoke C. democrat D. parashute E. Bible 7.____
8. A. existance B. enthusiasm C. medal D. sandwiches E. dunce 8.____
9. A. loyalty B. eternal C. chanceler D. psychology E. assessment 9.____
10. A. bungalow B. mutilate C. forcible D. ridiculous E. cawcus 10.____
11. A. lieutenant B. abandoned C. successor D. phisycal E. inquiries 11.____
12. A. nuisance B. coranation C. voluntary D. faculties E. awe 12.____
13. A. indipendance B. notwithstanding C. tariff D. opportue E. accompanying 13.____
14. A. statutes B. rhubarb C. corset D. prurient E. subsedy 14.____
15. A. partisan B. initiate C. colonel D. ilness E. errant 15.____
16. A. acquired B. wrapped C. propriater D. screech E. dune 16.____
17. A. sufrage B. countenance C. fraternally D. undo E. fireman 17.____
18. A. ladies B. chef C. spirituelist D. Sabbath E. itemized 18.____
19. A. ere B. interests C. cheesecloth D. paridoxical E. garish 19.____
20. A. bulletin B. neutral C. porttiere D. discretion E. inconvenienced 20.____

KEY (CORRECT ANSWERS)

1. D. conclusively
2. C. religious
3. E. cavalry
4. A. acknowledge
5. C. obstacles
6. B. burglaries
7. D. parachute
8. A. existence
9. C. chancellor
10. E. caucus
11. D. physical
12. B. coronation
13. A. independence
14. E. subsidy
15. D. illness
16. C. proprietor
17. A. suffrage
18. C. spiritualist
19. D. paradoxical
20. C. portiere

TEST 4

DIRECTIONS: In each question of the following tests, select the letter of the one MISSPELLED word in each of the listed groups of five (5) words. *PRINT THE LETTER OF THE CORRECT ANSWER IN THE SPACE AT THE RIGHT.*

1. A. I'd B. premises C. hysterics D. aparantly E. faculties 1.____
2. A. discipline B. ajurnment C. bachelor D. lose E. wrapped 2.____
3. A. simular B. bulletin C. lovable D. bored E. quizzes 3.____
4. A. attendance B. preparation C. refrigerator D. cafateria E. twelfth 4.____
5. A. inconvenienced B. courtesies C. raisin D. hosiery E. politicean 5.____
6. A. reccommendation B. colonel C. sandwiches D. women's E. undoubtedly 6.____
7. A. technical B. imediately C. temporarily D. dormitory E. voluntary 7.____
8. A. salaries B. abandoned C. consistent D. unconcious E. herald 8.____
9. A. duly B. leer C. emphasise D. vacant E. requisition 9.____
10. A. melancholy B. citrus C. omissions D. bazaar E. derigable 10.____
11. A. acquired B. mercury C. stetistics D. thought E. vassal 11.____
12. A. tempature B. calendar C. series D. gout E. alcohol 12.____
13. A. important B. foreigner C. Australia D. leggend E. rhythm 13.____
14. A. height B. achevement C. monarchial D. axle E. fertile 14.____
15. A. falsity B. prestige C. conquer D. arketecture E. Jerusalem 15.____
16. A. magnifecent B. bacteria C. holly D. diseases E. cellar 16.____
17. A. medicine B. grievous C. beaker D. benefits E. attendents 17.____
18. A. military B. vacancy C. weird D. feudalism E. hybird 18.____
19. A. adopted B. agrigate C. Renaissance D. tournament E. colonies 19.____
20. A. vivisection B. penitentiary C. candadacy D. seer E. Sabbath 20.____

109

KEY (CORRECT ANSWERS)

1. D. apparently
2. B. adjournment
3. A. similar
4. D. cafeteria
5. E. politician
6. A. recommendation
7. B. immediately
8. D. unconscious
9. C. emphasizes or emphasis
10. E. dirigible
11. C. statistics
12. A. temperature
13. D. legend
14. B. achievement
15. D. architecture
16. A. magnificent
17. E. attendants
18. E. hybrid
19. B. aggregate
20. C. candidacy

TEST 5

DIRECTIONS: In each question of the following tests, select the letter of the one MIS-SPELLED word in each of the listed groups of five (5) words. *PRINT THE LETTER OF THE CORRECT ANSWER IN THE SPACE AT THE RIGHT.*

1. A. acknowledging B. deligate C. foliage D. staid E. loot 1.____
2. A. gandar B. losing C. notwithstanding D. worlds E. torrent 2.____
3. A. medal B. utilize C. efficiency D. apricot E. soliceting 3.____
4. A. museum B. Christian C. possesion D. occasional E. bored 4.____
5. A. capitol B. sieze C. premises D. fragrance E. tonnage 5.____
6. A. requisition B. faculties C. canon D. chaufur E. stomach 6.____
7. A. solemn B. ascertain C. I'll D. chef E. delinquant 7.____
8. A. parliments B. distributor C. voluntary D. lovable E. counsel 8.____
9. A. morale B. democrat C. rhumatism D. dormitory E. leased 9.____
10. A. screech B. missapropriating C. courtesies D. wraith E. furlough 10.____
11. A. tryst B. tarriff C. visible D. accent E. contraries 11.____
12. A. dizzy B. leggings C. steak D. compaine E. interior 12.____
13. A. profit B. tiranny C. shocked D. response E. innocent 13.____
14. A. freshman B. vague C. larsiny D. ignorant E. worrying 14.____
15. A. disatesfied B. jealous C. unfortunately D. economical E. lettuce 15.____
16. A. based B. primarily C. condemned D. accompanied E. dupped 16.____
17. A. superntendant B. veil C. congenial D. quantities E. ere 17.____
18. A. unanimous B. dessert C. undoubtedly D. kolera E. nuisance 18.____
19. A. woman's B. bolero C. 'tis D. Pullman E. envellop 19.____
20. A. initiate B. grist C. pagent D. mention E. adieu 20.____

KEY (CORRECT ANSWERS)

1. B. delegate
2. A. gander
3. E. soliciting
4. C. possession
5. B. seize
6. D. chauffeur
7. E. delinquent
8. A. parliaments
9. C. rheumatism
10. B. misappropriating
11. B. tariff
12. D. campaign
13. B. tyranny
14. C. larceny
15. A. dissatisfied
16. E. duped
17. A. superintendent
18. D. cholera
19. E. envelope
20. C. pageant

TEST 6

DIRECTIONS: In each question of the following tests, select the letter of the one MISSPELLED word in each of the listed groups of five (5) words. *PRINT THE LETTER OF THE CORRECT ANSWER IN THE SPACE AT THE RIGHT.*

1. A. attach B. voucher C. twins D. assistence E. cordial 1.____
2. A. faculties B. people's C. indetedness D. ignorant E. resource 2.____
3. A. wholly B. apitite C. twelfth D. unauthorized E. embroider 3.____
4. A. certified B. attorneys C. foggy D. potato E. extravigent 4.____
5. A. hysterics B. simelar C. intelligent D. label E. salaries 5.____
6. A. apponants B. we're C. finely D. herald E. continuous 6.____
7. A. cancellation B. athletic C. perminant D. preference E. utilize 7.____
8. A. urns B. zephyr C. tuition D. incidentally E. aquisition 8.____
9. A. kinsaan B. bazaar C. foliage D. wretched E. asassination 9.____
10. A. insignia B. bimonthly C. typewriting D. notariety E. psychology 10.____
11. A. continually B. guild C. vegtable D. vague E. patience 11.____
12. A. desease B. parole C. gallery D. awkward E. you'd 12.____
13. A. border B. warrant C. operated D. economics E. ilegal 13.____
14. A. fatal B. agatation C. obliged D. studying E. resignation 14.____
15. A. ammendment B. promptness C. glimpse D. canon E. tract 15.____
16. A. wholly B. apricot C. destruction D. pappal E. leisure 16.____
17. A. issuing B. rabbid C. unusual D. parasite E. khaki 17.____
18. A. nowadays B. courtesies C. negotiate D. gaurdian E. derrick 18.____
19. A. partisan B. seanse C. vacancy D. fragrance E. corps 19.____
20. A. equipped B. nuisance C. phrenology D. foriegn E. insignia 20.____

KEY (CORRECT ANSWERS)

1. D. assistance
2. C. indebtedness
3. B. appetite
4. E. extravagant
5. B. similar
6. A. opponents
7. C. permanent
8. E. acquisition
9. E. assassination
10. D. notoriety
11. C. vegetable
12. A. disease
13. E. illegal
14. B. agitation
15. A. amendment
16. D. papal
17. B. rabid
18. D. guardian
19. B. eance
20. D. foreign

TEST 7

DIRECTIONS: In each question of the following tests, select the letter of the one MIS-SPELLED word in each of the listed groups of five (5) words. *PRINT THE LETTER OF THE CORRECT ANSWER IN THE SPACE AT THE RIGHT.*

1. A. frightfully   B. mantain   C. post office   D. specific   E. bachelor   1.____
2. A. cease   B. turkeys   C. woman's   D. hustling   E. weild   2.____
3. A. expidition   B. valuing   C. typhoid   D. grapevines E. advice   3.____
4. A. balance   B. visible   C. correspondant   D. etc.   E. arctic   4.____
5. A. benefit   B. arkives   C. classified   D. inasmuch   E. sincerity   5.____
6. A. obedient   B. vengeance   C. plague   D. fascinate   E. contageous 6.____
7. A. desicion   B. partner   C. economy   D. piece   E. arrogant   7.____
8. A. dyeing   B. lightning   C. millenary   D. undulate   E. embarrass   8.____
9. A. strenuous   B. isicle   C. panel   D. suburb   E. luxury   9.____
10. A. aisle   B. proffer   C. people's   D. condemed   E. morale   10.____
11. A. advising   B. recognizing   C. seize   D. supply   E. tradegy   11.____
12. A. intensive   B. stationary   C. benifit   D. equipped   E. preferring 12.____
13. A. predjudice   B. pervade   C. excel   D. capitol   E. chimera   13.____
14. A. all right   B. ninty   C. cronies   D. nervous   E. separate   14.____
15. A. atheletic   B. queue   C. schedule   D. furl   E. credible   15.____
16. A. inevitable   B. sincerly   C. monkeys   D. definite   E. cynical   16.____
17. A. niece   B. accommodate   C. loveliness   D. reciept   E. forcibly   17.____
18. A. cancel   B. chagrined   C. allies   D. playwright E. liutenant   18.____
19. A. pageant   B. alcohol   C. villian   D. Odyssey   E. criticize   19.____
20. A. acknowledge B. article   C. contemptible   D. taciturn   E. sovreign   20.____

KEY (CORRECT ANSWERS)

1. B. maintain
2. E. wield
3. A. expedition
4. C. correspondent
5. B. archives
6. E. contagious
7. A. decision
8. C. millinery
9. B. icicle
10. D. condemned
11. E. tragedy
12. C. benefit
13. A. prejudice
14. B. ninety
15. A. athletic
16. B. sincerely
17. D. receipt
18. E. lieutenant
19. C. villain
20. E. sovereign

TEST 8

DIRECTIONS: In each question of the following tests, select the letter of the one MISSPELLED word in each of the listed groups of five (5) words. *PRINT THE LETTER OF THE CORRECT ANSWER IN THE SPACE AT THE RIGHT.*

1. A. incurred   B. cieling   C. strengthen   D. carnage   E. typical   1.____
2. A. twins   B. year's   C. acutely   D. changible   E. facility   2.____
3. A. deliscious   B. enormous   C. likeness   D. witnesses   E. commodity   3.____
4. A. scenes   B. enlargement   C. discretion   D. acknowledging   E. sesion   4.____
5. A. annum   B. strenuous   C. tretchery   D. infamy   E. opportune   5.____
6. A. marmelade   B. loot   C. kinsman   D. crochet   E. hawser   6.____
7. A. sophmore   B. duly   C. across   D. lovable   E. propaganda   7.____
8. A. quantities   B. rickety   C. roommate   D. penetentiary   E. lose   8.____
9. A. interrupt   B. cauldron   C. convienient   D. successor   E. apiece   9.____
10. A. acquire   B. incesent   C. forfeit   D. typewritten   E. dysentery   10.____
11. A. inferred   B. whisle   C. jovial   D. conscript   E. gracious   11.____
12. A. tantalizing   B. ominous   C. conductor   D. duchess   E. telagram   12.____
13. A. reconcile   B. primitive   C. sausy   D. quinine   E. cede   13.____
14. A. immagine   B. viaduct   C. chisel   D. Saturn   E. currant   14.____
15. A. amplify   B. greace   C. cholera   D. perilous   E. theology   15.____
16. A. pursevere   B. deodorize   C. ligament   D. illuminate   E. dropsy   16.____
17. A. cavalier   B. transparent   C. perjury   D. vicinaty   E. navigate   17.____
18. A. postpone   B. dictaphone   C. corral   D. alligator   E. arteficial   18.____
19. A. cannon   B. hospital   C. distilliry   D. righteous   E. secession   19.____
20. A. matrimony   B. digestable   C. scrutiny   D. artisan   E. mediocre   20.____

KEY (CORRECT ANSWERS)

1. B. ceiling
2. D. changeable
3. A. delicious
4. E. session
5. C. treachery
6. A. marmalade
7. A. sophomore
8. D. penitentiary
9. C. convenient
10. B. incessant
11. B. whistle
12. E. telegram
13. C. saucy
14. A. imagine
15. B. grease
16. A. persevere
17. D. vicinity
18. E. artificial
19. C. distillery
20. B. digestible

TEST 9

DIRECTIONS: In each question of the following tests, select the letter of the one MISSPELLED word in each of the listed groups of five (5) words. *PRINT THE LETTER OF THE CORRECT ANSWER IN THE SPACE AT THE RIGHT.*

1. A. feirce B. ascent C. allies D. doctor E. coming 1._____
2. A. hopeless B. absense C. foretell D. certain E. similar 2._____
3. A. advise B. muscle C. manual D. provocation E. copywright 3._____
4. A. behooves B. reservoir C. frostbiten D. squalor E. ambuscade 4._____
5. A. systematic B. precious C. tremendos D. insulation E. brilliant 5._____
6. A. significant B. jurisdiction C. libel D. monkies E. legacy 6._____
7. A. dual B. authentic C. serenety D. mechanism E. suburban 7._____
8. A. candel B. dissolution C. laceration D. portend E. pigeon 8._____
9. A. loyalty B. periodic C. presume D. led E. suprano 9._____
10. A. mania B. medicinal C. dungarees D. overwelming E. masquerade 10._____
11. A. pitiful B. latter C. ommitted D. agreement E. reconcile 11._____
12. A. bananna B. routine C. likewise D. indecent E. habitually 12._____
13. A. relieve B. copys C. ninety D. crowded E. electoral 13._____
14. A. adviseable B. illustrative C. financial D. nevertheless E. chimneys 14._____
15. A. prisioner B. immediate C. statistics D. surgeon E. abscond 15._____
16. A. option B. extradite C. comparitive D. jealousy E. illusion 16._____
17. A. handicaped B. assurance C. sympathy D. speech E. dining 17._____
18. A. recommend B. carraige C. disapprove D. independent E. mortgage 18._____
19. A. systematic B. ingenuity C. tenet D. uncanny E. intrigueing 19._____
20. A. arduous B. hideous C. fervant D. companies E. breach 20._____

KEY (CORRECT ANSWERS)

1. A. fierce
2. B. absence
3. E. copyright
4. C. frostbitten
5. C. tremendous
6. D. monkeys
7. C. serenity
8. A. candle
9. E. soprano
10. D. overwhelming
11. C. omitted
12. A. banana
13. B. copies
14. A. advisable
15. A. prisoner
16. C. comparative
17. A. handicapped
18. B. carriage
19. E. intriguing
20. C. fervent

TEST 10

DIRECTIONS: In each question of the following tests, select the letter of the one MISSPELLED word in each of the listed groups of five (5) words. *PRINT THE LETTER OF THE CORRECT ANSWER IN THE SPACE AT THE RIGHT.*

1. A. together   B. attempt   C. loyalty   D. innocent   E. rinse   1.____
2. A. argueing   B. emergency   C. kindergarten D. religious   E. schedule   2.____
3. A. society   B. anticipate   C. dissatisfy   D. responsable   E. temporary   3.____
4. A. chaufeur   B. grammar   C. planned   D. dining room   E. accurate   4.____
5. A. confidence B. maturity   C. aspirations   D. evasion   E. insurence   5.____
6. A. unnecessary B. dirigible   C. transparant   D. similar   E. appetite   6.____
7. A. treachery   B. comedian   C. arrest   D. recollect   E. mistep   7.____
8. A. falsify   B. blight   C. flexible   D. drasticaly   E. meddlesome   8.____
9. A. congestion B. publickly   C. receipts   D. academic   E. paralyze   9.____
10. A. possibilities B. undergoes C. consistant   D. aggression   E. pledge   10.____
11. A. wrist   B. welfare   C. necessity   D. scenery   E. tendancy   11.____
12. A. commiting B. accusation   C. endurance   D. agreeable   E. excitable   12.____
13. A. despair   B. surgury   C. privilege   D. appreciation E. journeying   13.____
14. A. cameos   B. propaganda   C. delicious   D. heathen   E. interupt   14.____
15. A. relieve   B. disappear   C. development   D. matress   E. ninety-nine   15.____
16. A. finally   B. bullitin   C. doctor   D. desirable   E. sincerely   16.____
17. A. wrest   B. array   C. auspices   D. sacrafice   E. generations   17.____
18. A. liquid   B. vegetable   C. silence   D. familiar   E. fasinate   18.____
19. A. tomato   B. suspence   C. leisure   D. license   E. permanent   19.____
20. A. characteristic B. soliciting C. repitious   D. immediately   E. extravagant   20.____

KEY (CORRECT ANSWERS)

1. C. loyalty
2. A. arguing
3. D. responsible
4. A. chauffeur
5. E. insurance
6. C. transparent
7. E. misstep
8. D. drastically
9. B. publicly
10. C. consistent
11. E. tendency
12. A. committing
13. B. surgery
14. E. interrupt
15. D. mattress
16. B. bulletin
17. D. sacrifice
18. E. fascinate
19. B. suspense
20. C. repetitious

CLERICAL ABILITIES TEST
EXAMINATION SECTION
TEST 1

DIRECTIONS: Each question or incomplete statement is followed by several suggested answers or completions. Select the one that BEST answers the question or completes the statement. *PRINT THE LETTER OF THE CORRECT ANSWER IN THE SPACE AT THE RIGHT.*

Questions 1-10.

DIRECTIONS: Questions 1 through 10 consist of lines of names, dates, and numbers. For each question, you are to choose the option (A, B, C, or D) in Column II which EXACTLY matches the information in Column I. *PRINT THE LETTER OF THE CORRECT ANSWER IN THE SPACE AT THE RIGHT.*

SAMPLE QUESTION

Column I
Schneider 11/16/75 581932

Column II
A. Schneider 11/16/75 518932
B. Schneider 11/16/75 581932
C. Schnieder 11/16/75 581932
D. Shnieder 11/16/75 518932

The correct answer is B. Only Option B shows the name, date, and number exactly as they are in Column I. Option A has a mistake in the number. Option C has a mistake in the name. Option D has a mistake in the name and in the number. Now answer Questions 1 through 10 in the same manner.

Column I
1. Johnston 12/26/74 659251

Column II
A. Johnson 12/23/74 659251
B. Johston 12/26/74 659251
C. Johnston 12/26/74 695251
D. Johnston 12/26/74 659251

1.____

2. Allison 1/26/75 9939256

A. Allison 1/26/75 9939256
B. Alisson 1/26/75 9939256
C. Allison 1/26/76 9399256
D. Allison 1/26/75 9993356

2.____

3. Farrell 2/12/75 361251

A. Farell 2/21/75 361251
B. Farrell 2/12/75 361251
C. Farrell 2/21/75 361251
D. Farrell 2/12/75 361151

3.____

4. Guerrero 4/28/72 105689   A. Guererro 4/28/72 105689   4._____
                                 B. Guererro 4/28/72 105986
                                 C. Guererro 4/28/72 105869
                                 D. Guerrero 4/28/72 105689

5. McDonnell 6/05/73 478215   A. McDonnell 6/15/73 478215   5._____
                                 B. McDonnell 6/05/73 478215
                                 C. McDonnell 6/05/73 472815
                                 D. MacDonell 6/05/73 478215

6. Shepard 3/31/71 075421   A. Sheperd 3/31/71 075421   6._____
                                 B. Shepard 3/13/71 075421
                                 C. Shepard 3/31/71 075421
                                 D. Shepard 3/13/71 075241

7. Russell 4/01/69 031429   A. Russell 4/01/69 031429   7._____
                                 B. Russell 4/10/69 034129
                                 C. Russell 4/10/69 031429
                                 D. Russell 4/01/69 034129

8. Phillips 10/16/68 961042   A. Philipps 10/16/68 961042   8._____
                                 B. Phillips 10/16/68 960142
                                 C. Phillips 10/16/68 961042
                                 D. Philipps 10/16/68 916042

9. Campbell 11/21/72 624856   A. Campbell 11/21/72 624856   9._____
                                 B. Campbell 11/21/72 624586
                                 C. Campbell 11/21/72 624686
                                 D. Campbel 11/21/72 624856

10. Patterson 9/18/71 76199176 A. Patterson 9/18/72 76191976 10._____
                                 B. Patterson 9/18/71 76199176
                                 C. Patterson 9/18/72 76199176
                                 D. Patterson 9/18/71 76919176

Questions 11-15.

DIRECTIONS: Questions 11 through 15 consist of groups of numbers and letters which you are to compare. For each question, you are to choose the option (A, B, C, or D) in Column I which EXACTLY matches the group of numbers and letters given in Column I.

SAMPLE QUESTION

Column I   Column II
B92466   A. B92644
                  B. B94266
                  C. A92466
                  D. B92466

3 (#1)

The correct answer is D. Only Option D in Column II shows the group of numbers and letters EXACTLY as it appears in Column I. Now answer Questions 11 through 15 in the same manner.

    Column I   Column II

11. 925AC5
    A. 952CA5
    B. 925AC5
    C. 952AC5
    D. 925CA6

11.____

12. Y006925
    A. Y060925
    B. Y006295
    C. Y006529
    D. Y006925

12.____

13. J236956
    A. J236956
    B. J326965
    C. J239656
    D. J932656

13.____

14. AB6952
    A. AB6952
    B. AB9625
    C. AB9652
    D. AB6925

14.____

15. X259361
    A. X529361
    B. X259631
    C. X523961
    D. X259361

15.____

Questions 16-25.

DIRECTIONS: Each of questions 16 through 25 consists of three lines of code letters and three lines of numbers. The numbers on each line should correspond with the code letters on the same line in accordance with the table below.

Code Letter	S	V	W	A	Q	M	X	E	G	K
Corresponding Number	0	1	2	3	4	5	5	7	8	9

On some of the lines, an error exists in the coding. Compare the letters and numbers in each question carefully. If you find an error or errors on:
    only one of the lines in the question, mark your answer A;
    any two lines in the question, mark your answer B;
    all three lines in the question, mark your answer C;
    none of the lines in the question, mark your answer D.

SAMPLE QUESTION

WQGKSXG	2489068
XEKVQMA	6591453
KMAESXV	9527061

In the above sample, the first line is correct since each code letter listed has the correct corresponding number. On the second line, an error exists because code letter E should have the number 7 instead of the number 5. On the third line, an error exists because the code letter A should have the number 3 instead of the number 2. Since there are errors in two of the three lines, the correct answer is B. Now answer Questions 16 through 25 in the same manner.

16. SWQEKGA   0247983   16.____
      KEAVSXM   9731065
      SSAXGKQ   0036894

17. QAMKMVS   4259510   17.____
      MGGEASX   5897306
      KSWMKWS   9125920

18. WKXQWVE   2964217   18.____
      QKXXQVA   4966413
      AWMXGVS   3253810

19. GMMKASE   8559307   19.____
      AWVSKSW   3210902
      QAVSVGK   4310189

20. XGKQSMK   6894049   20.____
      QSVKEAS   4019730
      GSMXKMV   8057951

21. AEKMWSG   3195208   21.____
      MKQSVQK   5940149
      XGQAEVW   6843712

22. XGMKAVS   6858310   22.____
      SKMAWEQ   0953174
      GVMEQSA   8167403

23. VQSKAVE   1489317   23.____
      WQGKAEM   2489375
      MEGKAWQ   5689324

24. XMQVSKG   6541098   24.____
      QMEKEWS   4579720
      KMEVGKG   9571983

25. GKVAMEW   88912572   25._____
    AXMVKAE   3651937
    KWAGMAV   9238531

Questions 26-35.

DIRECTIONS: Each of Questions 26 through 35 consists of a column of figures. For each question, add the column of figures and choose the correct answer from the four choices given.

26. 5,665.43   26._____
     2,356.69
     6,447.24
     7,239.65

     A. 20,698.01   B. 21,709.01
     C. 21,718.01   D. 22,609.01

27. 817,209.55   27._____
     264,354.29
      82,368.76
     849,964.89

     A. 1,893.977.49   B. 1,989,988.39
     C. 2,009,077.39   D. 2,013,897.49

28. 156,366.89   28._____
     249,973.23
     823,229.49
      56,869.45

     A. 1,286,439.06   B. 1,287,521.06
     C. 1,297,539.06   D. 1,296,421.06

29.   23,422.15   29._____
     149,696.24
     238,377.53
      86,289.79
     505,533.63

     A. 989,229.34   B. 999,879.34
     C. 1,003,330.34   D. 1,023,329.34

30. 2,468,926.70   30.____
      656,842.28
       49,723.15
      832,369.59

    A. 3,218,062.72   B. 3,808,092.72
    C. 4,007,861.72   D. 4,818,192.72

31.   524,201.52   31.____
      7,775,678.51
      8,345,299.63
     40,628,898.08
     31,374,670.07

    A. 88,646,647.81   B. 88,646,747.91
    C. 88,648,647.91   D. 88,648,747.81

32. 6,824,829.40   32.____
       682,482.94
     5,542,015.27
       775,678.51
     7,732,507.25

    A. 21,557,513.37   B. 21,567,513.37
    C. 22,567,503.37   D. 22,567,513.37

33. 22,109,405.58   33.____
      6,097,093.43
      5,050,073.99
      8,118,050.05
      4,313,980.82

    A. 45,688,593.87   B. 45,688,603.87
    C. 45,689,593.87   D. 45,689,603.87

34. 79,324,114.19   34.____
     99,848,129.74
     43,331,653.31
     41,610,207.14

    A. 264,114,104.38   B. 264,114,114.38
    C. 265,114,114.38   D. 265,214,104.38

35. 33,729,653.94
     5,959,342.58
    26,052,715.47
     4,452,669.52
     7,079,953.59

    A. 76,374,334.10   B. 76,375,334.10
    C. 77,274,335.10   D. 77,275,335.10

35.____

Questions 36-40.

DIRECTIONS: Each of Questions 36 through 40 consists of a single number in Column I and four options in Column II. For each question, you are to choose the option (A, B, C, or D) in Column II which EXACTLY matches the number in Column I.

SAMPLE QUESTION

Column I   Column II
5965121   A. 5956121
                  B. 5965121
                  C. 5966121
                  D. 5965211

The correct answer is B. Only Option B shows the number EXACTLY as it appears in Column I. Now answer Questions 36 through 40 in the same manner.

Column I   Column II
36. 9643242   A. 9643242
                        B. 9462342
                        C. 9642442
                        D. 9463242

36.____

37. 3572477   A. 3752477
                        B. 3725477
                        C. 3572477
                        D. 3574277

37.____

38. 5276101   A. 5267101
                        B. 5726011
                        C. 5271601
                        D. 5276101

38.____

39. 4469329   A. 4496329
                        B. 4469329
                        C. 4496239
                        D. 4469239

39.____

40. 2326308

A. 2236308
B. 2233608
C. 2326308
D. 2323608

40.____

KEY (CORRECT ANSWERS)

1.	D	11.	B	21.	A	31.	D
2.	A	12.	D	22.	C	32.	A
3.	B	13.	A	23.	B	33.	B
4.	D	14.	A	24.	D	34.	A
5.	B	15.	D	25.	A	35.	C
6.	C	16.	D	26.	B	36.	A
7.	A	17.	C	27.	D	37.	C
8.	C	18.	A	28.	A	38.	D
9.	A	19.	D	29.	C	39.	B
10.	B	20.	B	30.	C	40.	C

TEST 2

DIRECTIONS: Each question or incomplete statement is followed by several suggested answers or completions. Select the one that BEST answers the question or completes the statement. *PRINT THE LETTER OF THE CORRECT ANSWER IN THE SPACE AT THE RIGHT.*

Questions 1-5.

DIRECTIONS: Each of Questions 1 through 5 consists of a name and a dollar amount. In each question, the name and dollar amount in Column II should be an EXACT copy of the name and dollar amount in Column I. If there is:
a mistake only in the name, mark your answer A;
a mistake only in the dollar amount, mark your answer B;
a mistake in both the name and the dollar amount, mark your answer C;
no mistake in either the name or the dollar amount, mark your answer D.

SAMPLE QUESTION

Column I	Column II
George Peterson	George Petersson
$125.50	$125.50

Compare the name and dollar amount in Column II with the name and dollar amount in Column I. The name *Petersson* in Column II is spelled *Peterson* in Column I. The amount is the same in both columns. Since there is a mistake only in the name, the answer to the sample question is A. Now answer Questions 1 through 5 in the same manner.

	Column I	Column II	
1.	Susanne Shultz $3440	Susanne Schultz $3440	1.____
2.	Anibal P. Contrucci $2121.61	Anibel P. Contrucci $2112.61	2.____
3.	Eugenio Mendoza $12.45	Eugenio Mendozza $12.45	3.____
4.	Maurice Gluckstadt $4297	Maurice Gluckstadt $4297	4.____
5.	John Pampellonne $4656.94	John Pammpellonne $4566.94	5.____

Questions 6-11.

DIRECTIONS: Each of Questions 6 through 11 consist of a set of names and addresses, which you are to compare. In each question, the name and addresses in Column II should be an EXACT copy of the name and address in Column I. If there is:
- a mistake only in the name, mark your answer A;
- a mistake only in the address, mark your answer B;
- a mistake in both the name and address, mark your answer C;
- no mistake in either the name or address, mark your answer D.

SAMPLE QUESTION

Column I
Michael Filbert
456 Reade Street
New York, N.Y. 10013

Column II
Michael Filbert
645 Reade Street
New York, N.Y. 10013

Since there is a mistake only in the address (the street number should be 456 instead of 645), the answer to the sample question is B. Now answer Questions 6 through 11 in the same manner.

	Column I	Column II	
6.	Hilda Goettelmann 55 Lenox Rd. Brooklyn, N.Y. 11226	Hilda Goettelman 55 Lenox Ave. Brooklyn, N.Y. 11226	6.____
7.	Arthur Sherman 2522 Batchelder St. Brooklyn, N.Y. 11235	Arthur Sharman 2522 Batcheder St. Brooklyn, N.Y. 11253	7.____
8.	Ralph Barnett 300 West 28 Street New York, New York 10001	Ralph Barnett 300 West 28 Street New York, New York 10001	8.____
9.	George Goodwin 135 Palmer Avenue Staten Island, New York 10302	George Godwin 135 Palmer Avenue Staten Island, New York 10302	9.____
10.	Alonso Ramirez 232 West 79 Street New York, N.Y. 10024	Alonso Ramirez 223 West 79 Street New York, N.Y. 10024	10.____
11.	Cynthia Graham 149-34 83 Street Howard Beach, N.Y. 11414	Cynthia Graham 149-35 83 Street Howard Beach, N.Y. 11414	11.____

Questions 12-20.

DIRECTIONS: Questions 12 through 20 are problems in subtraction. For each question do the subtraction and select your answer from the four choices given.

12. 232,921.85
     -179,587.68

    A. 52,433.17   B. 52,434.17
    C. 53,334.17   D. 53,343,17

12.____

13. 5,531,876.29
     -3,897,158.36

    A. 1,634,717.93   B. 1,644,718.93
    C. 1,734,717.93   D. 1,7234,718.93

13.____

14. 1,482,658.22
     -937,925.76

    A. 544,633.46   B. 544,732.46
    C. 545,632.46   D. 545,732.46

14.____

15. 937,828.17
     -259,673.88

    A. 678,154.29   B. 679,154.29
    C. 688,155.39   D. 699,155.39

15.____

16. 760,412.38
     -263,465.95

    A. 496,046.43   B. 496,946.43
    C. 496,956.43   D. 497,046.43

16.____

17. 3,203,902.26
     -2,933,087.96

    A. 260,814.30   B. 269,824.30
    C. 270,814.30   D. 270,824.30

17.____

18. 1,023,468.71
     -934,678.88

    A. 88,780.83   B. 88,789.83
    C. 88,880.83   D. 88,889.83

18.____

19. 831,549.47
    -772,814.78

    A. 58,734.69   B. 58,834.69
    C. 59,735.69   D. 59,834.69

20. 6,306,181.74
    -3,617,376.99

    A. 2,687,904.99   B. 2,688,904.99
    C. 2,689,804.99   D. 2,799,905.99

Questions 21-30.

DIRECTIONS: Each of Questions 21 through 30 consists of three lines of code letters and three lines of numbers. The numbers on each line should correspond with the code letters on the same line in accordance with the table below.

Code Letter	J	U	B	T	Y	D	K	R	L	P
Corresponding Number	0	1	2	3	4	5	5	7	8	9

On some of the lines, an error exists in the coding. Compare the letters and numbers in each question carefully. If you find an error or errors on:
only *one* of the lines in the question, mark your answer A;
any *two* lines in the question, mark your answer B;
all *three* lines in the question, mark your answer C;
none of the lines in the question, mark your answer D.

SAMPLE QUESTION

BJRPYUR   2079417
DTBPYKJ   5328460
YKLDBLT   4685283

In the above sample, the first line is correct since each code letter listed has the correct corresponding number. On the second line, an error exists because code letter P should have the number 9 instead of the number 8. The third line is correct since each code letter listed has the correct corresponding number. Since there is an error in *one* of the three lines, the correct answer is A. Now answer Questions 21 through 30 in the same manner.

21. BYPDTJL   2495308
    PLRDTJU   9815301
    DTJRYLK   5207486

22. RPBYRJK   7934706
    PKTYLBU   9624821
    KDLPJYR   6489047

5 (#2)

23.	TPYBUJR	3942107	23.____
	BYRKPTU	2476931	
	DUKPYDL	5169458	
24.	KBYDLPL	6345898	24.____
	BLRKBRU	2876261	
	JTULDYB	0318542	
25.	LDPYDKR	8594567	25.____
	BDKDRJL	2565708	
	BDRPLUJ	2679810	
26.	PLRLBPU	9858291	26.____
	LPYKRDJ	88936750	
	TDKPDTR	3569527	
27.	RKURPBY	7617924	27.____
	RYUKPTJ	7426930	
	RTKPTJD	7369305	
28.	DYKPBJT	5469203	28.____
	KLPJBTL	6890238	
	TKPLBJP	3698209	
29.	BTPRJYL	2397148	29.____
	LDKUTYR	8561347	
	YDBLRPJ	4528190	
30.	ULPBKYT	1892643	30.____
	KPDTRBJ	6953720	
	YLKJPTB	4860932	

KEY (CORRECT ANSWERS)

1.	A	11.	D	21.	B
2.	C	12.	C	22.	C
3.	A	13.	A	23.	D
4.	D	14.	B	24.	B
5.	C	15.	A	25.	A
6.	C	16.	B	26.	C
7.	C	17.	C	27.	A
8.	D	18.	B	28.	D
9.	A	19.	A	29.	B
10.	B	20.	B	30.	D

RECORD KEEPING
EXAMINATION SECTION
TEST 1

DIRECTIONS: Each question or incomplete statement is followed by several suggested answers or completions. Select the one that BEST answers the question or completes the statement. *PRINT THE LETTER OF THE CORRECT ANSWER IN THE SPACE AT THE RIGHT.*

Questions 1-7.

DIRECTIONS: In answering Questions 1 through 7, use the following master list. For each question, determine where the name would fit on the master list. Each answer choice indicates right before or after the name in the answer choice.

    Aaron, Jane
    Armstead, Brendan
    Bailey, Charles
    Dent, Ricardo
    Grant, Mark
    Mars, Justin
    Methieu, Justine
    Parker, Cathy
    Sampson, Suzy
    Thomas, Heather

1. Schmidt, William
   A. Right before Cathy Parker
   B. Right after Heather Thomas
   C. Right after Suzy Sampson
   D. Right before Ricardo Dent

2. Asanti, Kendall
   A. Right before Jane Aaron
   B. Right after Charles Bailey
   C. Right before Justine Methieu
   D. Right after Brendan Armstead

3. O'Brien, Daniel
   A. Right after Justine Methieu
   B. Right before Jane Aaron
   C. Right after Mark Grant
   D. Right before Suzy Sampson

4. Marrow, Alison
   A. Right before Cathy Parker
   B. Right before Justin Mars
   C. Right before Mark Grant
   D. Right after Heather Thomas

5. Grantt, Marissa
   A. Right before Mark Grant
   B. Right after Mark Grant
   C. Right after Justin Mars
   D. Right before Suzy Sampson

1.____

2.____

3.____

4.____

5.____

6. Thompson, Heath   6._____
   A. Right after Justin Mars   B. Right before Suzy Sampson
   C. Right after Heather Thomas   D. Right before Cathy Parker

DIRECTIONS: Before answering Question 7, add in all of the names from Questions 1 through 6. Then fit the name in alphabetical order based on the new list.

7. Francisco, Mildred   7._____
   A. Right before Mark Grant   B. Right after Marissa Grantt
   C. Right before Alison Marrow   D. Right after Kendall Asanti

Questions 8-10.

DIRECTIONS: In answering Questions 8 through 10, compare each pair of names and addresses. Indicate whether they are the same or different in any way.

8. William H. Pratt, J.D.   William H. Pratt, J.D.   8._____
   Attourney at Law   Attorney at Law
   A. No differences   B. 1 difference
   C. 2 differences   D. 3 differences

9. 1303 Theater Drive,; Apt. 3-B   1330 Theatre Drive,; Apt. 3-B   9._____
   A. No differences   B. 1 difference
   C. 2 differences   D. 3 differences

10. Petersdorff, Briana and Mary   Petersdorff, Briana and Mary   10._____
    A. No differences   B. 1 difference
    C. 2 differences   D. 3 differences

11. Which of the following words, if any, are misspelled?   11._____
    A. Affordable   B. Circumstansial
    C. Legalese   D. None of the above

Questions 12-13.

DIRECTIONS: Questions 12 and 13 are to be answered on the basis of the following table.

Standardized Test Results for High School Students in District #1230

	English	Math	Science	Reading
High School 1	21	22	15	18
High School 2	12	16	13	15
High School 3	16	18	21	17
High School 4	19	14	15	16

The scores for each high school in the district were averaged out and listed for each subject tested. Scores of 0-10 are significantly below College Readiness Standards. 11-15 are below College Readiness, 16-20 meet College Readiness, and 21-25 are above College Readiness.

12. If the high schools need to meet or exceed in at least half the categories in order to NOT be considered "at risk," which schools are considered "at risk"? 12.____
    A. High School 2
    B. High School 3
    C. High School 4
    D. Both A and C

13. What percentage of subjects did the district as a whole meet or exceed College Readiness standards? 13.____
    A. 25%
    B. 50%
    C. 75%
    D. 100%

Questions 14-15.

DIRECTIONS: Questions 14 and 15 are to be answered on the basis of the following information.

You have seven employees working as a part of your team: Austin, Emily, Jeremy, Christina, Martin, Harriet, and Steve. You have just sent an e-mail informing them that there will be a mandatory training session next week. To ensure that work still gets done, you are offering the training twice during the week: once on Tuesday and also on Thursday. This way half the employees will still be working while the other half attend the training. The only other issue is that Jeremy doesn't work on Tuesdays and Harriet doesn't work on Thursdays due to compressed work schedules.

14. Which of the following is a possible attendance roster for the first training session? 14.____
    A. Emily, Jeremy, Steve
    B. Steve, Christina, Harriet
    C. Harriet, Jeremy, Austin
    D. Steve, Martin, Jeremy

15. If Harriet, Christina, and Steve attend the training session on Tuesday, which of the following is a possible roster for Thursday's training session? 15.____
    A. Jeremy, Emily, and Austin
    B. Emily, Martin, and Harriet
    C. Austin, Christina, and Emily
    D. Jeremy, Emily, and Steve

Questions 16-20.

DIRECTIONS: In answering Questions 16 through 20, you will be given a word and will need to choose the answer choice that is MOST similar or different to the word.

16. Which word means the SAME as *annual*? 16.____
    A. Monthly
    B. Usually
    C. Yearly
    D. Constantly

17. Which word means the SAME as *effort*? 17.____
    A. Energy
    B. Equate
    C. Cherish
    D. Commence

18. Which word means the OPPOSITE of *forlorn*? 18.____
    A. Neglected
    B. Lethargy
    C. Optimistic
    D. Astonished

19. Which word means the SAME as *risk*? 19.____
    A. Admire
    B. Hazard
    C. Limit
    D. Hesitant

4 (#1)

20. Which word means the OPPOSITE of *translucent*? 20.____
    A. Opaque B. Transparent C. Luminous D. Introverted

21. Last year, Jamie's annual salary was $50,000. Her boss called her today 21.____
    to inform her that she would receive a 20% raise for the upcoming year. How
    much more money will Jamie receive next year?
    A. $60,000 B. $10,000 C. $1,000 D. $51,000

22. You and a co-worker work for a temp hiring agency as part of their office 22.____
    staff. You both are given 6 days off per month. How many days off are you
    and your co-worker given in a year?
    A. 24 B. 72 C. 144 D. 48

23. If Margot makes $34,000 per year and she works 40 hours per week for 23.____
    all 52 weeks, what is her hourly rate?
    A. $16.34/hour B. $17.00/hour C. $15.54/hour D. $13.23/hour

24. How many dimes are there in $175.00? 24.____
    A. 175 B. 1,750 C. 3,500 D. 17,500

25. If Janey is three times as old as Emily, and Emily is 3, how old is Janey? 25.____
    A. 6 B. 9 C. 12 D. 15

KEY (CORRECT ANSWERS)

1. C 11. B
2. D 12. A
3. A 13. D
4. B 14. B
5. B 15. A

6. C 16. C
7. A 17. A
8. B 18. C
9. C 19. B
10. A 20. A

21. B
22. C
23. A
24. B
25. B

TEST 2

DIRECTIONS: Each question or incomplete statement is followed by several suggested answers or completions. Select the one that BEST answers the question or completes the statement. *PRINT THE LETTER OF THE CORRECT ANSWER IN THE SPACE AT THE RIGHT.*

Questions 1-6.

DIRECTIONS: Questions 1 through 6 are to be answered on the basis of the following information.

item	name of item to be ordered
quantity	minimum number that can be ordered
beginning amount	amount in stock at start of month
amount received	amount receiving during month
ending amount	amount in stock at end of month
amount used	amount used during month
amount to order	will need at least as much of each item as used in the previous month
unit price	cost of each unit of an item
total price	total price for the order

Item	Quantity	Beginning	Received	Ending	Amount Used	Amount to Order	Unit Price	Total Price
Pens	10	22	10	8	24	20	$0.11	$2.20
Spiral notebooks	8	30	13	12			$0.25	
Binder clips	2 boxes	3 boxes	1 box	1 box			$1.79	
Sticky notes	3 packs	12 packs	4 packs	2 packs			$1.29	
Dry erase markers	1 pack (dozen)	34 markers	8 markers	40 markers			$16.49	
Ink cartridges (printer)	1 cartridge	3 cartridges	1 cartridge	2 cartridges			$79.99	
Folders	10 folders	25 folders	15 folders	10 folders			$1.08	

1. How many packs of sticky notes were used during the month?   1.____
   A. 16   B. 10   C. 12   D. 14

2. How many folders need to be ordered for next month?   2.____
   A. 15   B. 20   C. 30   D. 40

3. What is the total price of notebooks that you will need to order?   3.____
   A. $6.00   B. $0.25   C. $4.50   D. $2.75

4. Which of the following will you spend the second most money on?   4.____
   A. Ink cartridges   B. Dry erase markers
   C. Sticky notes   D. Binder clips

5. How many packs of dry erase markers should you order?   5.____
   A. 1   B. 8   C. 12   D. 0

6. What will be the total price of the file folders you order? 6._____
   A. $20.16 B. $21.60 C. $10.80 D. $4.32

Questions 7-11.

DIRECTIONS: Questions 7 through 11 are to be answered on the basis of the following table.

| Number of Car Accidents, By Location and Cause, for 2014 |||||||
| Cause | Location 1 || Location 2 || Location 3 ||
	Number	Percent	Number	Percent	Number	Percent
Severe Weather	10		25		30	
Excessive Speeding	20	40	5		10	
Impaired Driving	15		15	25	8	
Miscellaneous	5		15		2	4
TOTALS	50	100	60	100	50	100

7. Which of the following is the third highest cause of accidents for all three locations? 7._____
   A. Severe Weather
   B. Impaired Driving
   C. Miscellaneous
   D. Excessive Speeding

8. The average number of Severe Weather accidents per week at Location 3 for the year (52 weeks) was MOST NEARLY 8._____
   A. 0.57 B. 30 C. 1 D. 1.25

9. Which location had the LARGEST percentage of accidents caused by Impaired Driving? 9._____
   A. 1 B. 2 C. 3 D. Both A and B

10. If one-third of the accidents at all three locations resulted in at least one fatality, what is the LEAST amount of deaths caused by accidents last year? 10._____
    A. 60 B. 106 C. 66 D. 53

11. What is the percentage of accidents caused by miscellaneous means from all three locations in 2014? 11._____
    A. 5% B. 10% C. 13% D. 25%

12. How many pairs of the following groups of letters are exactly alike? 12._____
    ACDOBJ   ACDBOJ
    HEWBWR   HEWRWB
    DEERVS   DEERVS
    BRFQSX   BRFQSX
    WEYRVB   WEYRVB
    SPQRZA   SQRPZA

    A. 2 B. 3 C. 4 D. 5

Questions 13-19.

DIRECTIONS: Questions 13 through 19 are to be answered on the basis of the following information.

In 2012, the most current information on the American population was finished. The information was compiled by 200 volunteers in each of the 50 states. The territory of Puerto Rico, a sovereign of the United States, had 25 people assigned to compile data. In February of 2010, volunteers in each state and sovereign began collecting information. In Puerto Rico, data collection finished by January 31st, 2011, while work in the United States was completed on June 30, 2012. Each volunteer gathered data on the population of their state or sovereign. When the information was compiled, volunteers sent reports to the nation's capital, Washington, D.C. Each volunteer worked 20 hours per month and put together 10 reports per month. After the data was compiled in total, 50 people reviewed the data and worked from January 2012 to December 2012.

13. How many reports were generated from February 2010 to April 2010 in Illinois and Ohio?
    A. 3,000   B. 6,000   C. 12,000   D. 15,000

14. How many volunteers in total collected population data in January 2012?
    A. 10,000   B. 2,000   C. 225   D. 200

15. How many reports were put together in May 2012?
    A. 2,000   B. 50,000   C. 100,000   D. 100,250

16. How many hours did the Puerto Rican volunteers work in the fall (September-November)?
    A. 60   B. 500   C. 1,500   D. 0

17. How many workers were compiling or reviewing data in July 2012?
    A. 25   B. 50   C. 200   D. 250

18. What was the total amount of hours worked by Nevada volunteers in July 2010?
    A. 500   B. 4,000   C. 4,500   D. 5,000

19. How many reviewers worked in January 2013?
    A. 75   B. 50   C. 0   D. 25

20. John has to file 10 documents per shelf. How many documents would it take for John to fill 40 shelves?
    A. 40   B. 400   C. 4,500   D. 5,000

21. Jill wants to travel from New York City to Los Angeles by bike, which is approximately 2,772 miles. How many miles per day would Jill need to average if she wanted to complete the trip in 4 weeks?
    A. 100   B. 89   C. 99   D. 94

22. If there are 24 CPU's and only 7 monitors, how many more monitors do you need to have the same amount of monitors as CPU's?

22._____

    A. Not enough information   B. 17
    C. 31   D. 0

23. If Gerry works 5 days a week and 8 hours each day, and John works 3 days a week and 10 hours each day, how many more hours per year will Gerry work than John?

23._____

    A. They work the same amount of hours.
    B. 450
    C. 520
    D. 832

24. Jimmy gets transferred to a new office. The new office has 25 employees, but only 16 are there due to a blizzard. How many coworkers was Jimmy able to meet on his first day?

24._____

    A. 16   B. 25   C. 9   D. 7

25. If you do a fundraiser for charities in your area and raise $500 total, how much would you give to each charity if you were donating equal amounts to 3 of them?

25._____

    A. $250.00   B. $167.77   C. $50.00   D. $111.11

KEY (CORRECT ANSWERS)

1.	D		11.	C
2.	B		12.	B
3.	A		13.	C
4.	C		14.	A
5.	D		15.	C
6.	B		16.	C
7.	D		17.	B
8.	A		18.	B
9.	A		19.	C
10.	D		20.	B

21. C
22. B
23. C
24. A
25. B

TEST 3

DIRECTIONS: Each question or incomplete statement is followed by several suggested answers or completions. Select the one that BEST answers the question or completes the statement. *PRINT THE LETTER OF THE CORRECT ANSWER IN THE SPACE AT THE RIGHT.*

Questions 1-3.

DIRECTIONS: In answering Questions 1 through 3, choose the correctly spelled word.

1. A. allusion B. alusion C. allusien D. allution   1.____
2. A. altitude B. alltitude C. atlitude D. altlitude   2.____
3. A. althogh B. allthough C. althrough D. although   3.____

Questions 4-9.

DIRECTIONS: In answering Questions 4 through 9, choose the answer that BEST completes the analogy.

4. Odometer is to mileage as compass is to   4.____
   A. speed B. needle C. hiking D. direction

5. Marathon is to race as hibernation is to   5.____
   A. winter B. dream C. sleep D. bear

6. Cup is to coffee as bowl is to   6.____
   A. dish B. spoon C. food D. soup

7. Flow is to river as stagnant is to   7.____
   A. pool B. rain C. stream D. canal

8. Paw is to cat as hoof is to   8.____
   A. lamb B. horse C. lion D. elephant

9. Architect is to building as sculptor is to   9.____
   A. museum B. chisel C. stone D. statue

Questions 10-14.

DIRECTIONS: Questions 10 through 14 are to be answered on the basis of the following graph.

Population of Carroll City Broken Down by Age and Gender (in Thousands)			
Age	Female	Male	Total
Under 15	60	60	120
15-23		22	
24-33		20	44
34-43	13	18	31
44-53	20		67
64 and Over	65	65	130
TOTAL	230	232	462

10. How many people in the city are between the ages of 15-23?
    A. 70   B. 46,000   C. 70,000   D. 225,000

11. Approximately what percentage of the total population of the city was female aged 24-33?
    A. 10%   B. 5%   C. 15%   D. 25%

12. If 33% of the males have a job and 55% of females don't have a job, which of the following statements is TRUE?
    A. Males have approximately 2,600 more jobs than females.
    B. Females have approximately 49,000 more jobs than males.
    C. Females have approximately 26,000 more jobs than males.
    D. None of the above statements are true.

13. How many females between the ages of 15-23 live in Carroll City?
    A. 67,000   B. 24,000   C. 48,000   D. 91,000

14. Assume all males 44-53 living in Carroll City are employed. If two-thirds of males age 44-53 work jobs outside of Carroll City, how many work within city limits?
    A. 31,333
    B. 15,667
    C. 47,000
    D. Cannot answer the question with the information provided

Questions 15-16.

DIRECTIONS: Questions 15 and 16 are labeled as shown. Alphabetize them for filing. Choose the answer that correctly shows the order.

15. (1) AED
    (2) OOS
    (3) FOA
    (4) DOM
    (5) COB

    A. 2-5-4-3-2   B. 1-4-5-2-3   C. 1-5-4-2-3   D. 1-5-4-3-2

16. Alphabetize the names of the people. Last names are given last.
    (1) Lindsey Jamestown
    (2) Jane Alberta
    (3) Ally Jamestown
    (4) Allison Johnston
    (5) Lyle Moreno

    A. 2-1-3-4-5   B. 3-4-2-1-5   C. 2-3-1-4-5   D. 4-3-2-1-5

17. Which of the following words is misspelled?
    A. disgust
    B. whisper
    C. locale
    D. none of the above

Questions 18-21.

DIRECTIONS: Questions 18 through 21 are to be answered on the basis of the following list of employees.

    Robertson, Aaron
    Bacon, Gina
    Jerimiah, Trace
    Gillette, Stanley
    Jacks, Sharon

18. Which employee name would come in third in alphabetized list?
    A. Robertson, Aaron
    B. Jerimiah, Trace
    C. Gillette, Stanley
    D. Jacks, Sharon

19. Which employee's first name starts with the letter in the alphabet that is five letters after the first letter of their last name?
    A. Jerimiah, Trace
    B. Bacon, Gina
    C. Jacks, Sharon
    D. Gillette, Stanley

20. How many employees have last names that are exactly five letters long?
    A. 1   B. 2   C. 3   D. 4

21. How many of the employees have either a first or last name that starts with the letter "G"? 21._____
    A. 1 B. 2 C. 4 D. 5

Questions 22-25.

DIRECTIONS: Questions 22 through 25 are to be answered on the basis of the following chart.

Bicycle Sales (Model #34JA32)							
Country	May	June	July	August	September	October	Total
Germany	34	47	45	54	56	60	296
Britain	40	44	36	47	47	46	260
Ireland	37	32	32	32	34	33	200
Portugal	14	14	14	16	17	14	89
Italy	29	29	28	31	29	31	177
Belgium	22	24	24	26	25	23	144
Total	176	198	179	206	208	207	1166

22. What percentage of the overall total was sold to the German importer? 22._____
    A. 25.3% B. 22% C. 24.1% D. 23%

23. What percentage of the overall total was sold in September? 23._____
    A. 24.1% B. 25.6% C. 17.9% D. 24.6%

24. What is the average number of units per month imported into Belgium over the first four months shown? 24._____
    A. 26 B. 20 C. 24 D. 31

25. If you look at the three smallest importers, what is their total import percentage? 25._____
    A. 35.1% B. 37.1% C. 40% D. 28%

KEY (CORRECT ANSWERS)

1.	A	11.	B
2.	A	12.	C
3.	D	13.	C
4.	D	14.	B
5.	C	15.	D
6.	D	16.	C
7.	A	17.	D
8.	B	18.	D
9.	D	19.	B
10.	C	20.	B

21.	B
22.	A
23.	C
24.	C
25.	A

TEST 4

DIRECTIONS: Each question or incomplete statement is followed by several suggested answers or completions. Select the one that BEST answers the question or completes the statement. *PRINT THE LETTER OF THE CORRECT ANSWER IN THE SPACE AT THE RIGHT.*

Questions 1-6.

DIRECTIONS: In answering Questions 1 through 6, choose the sentence that represents the BEST example of English grammar.

1.
   A. Joey and me want to go on a vacation next week.
   B. Gary told Jim he would need to take some time off.
   C. If turning six years old, Jim's uncle would teach Spanish to him.
   D. Fax a copy of your resume to Ms. Perez and me.

   1.____

2.
   A. Jerry stood in line for almost two hours.
   B. The reaction to my engagement was less exciting than I thought it would be.
   C. Carlos and me have done great work on this project.
   D. Two parts of the speech needs to be revised before tomorrow.

   2.____

3.
   A. Arriving home, the alarm was tripped.
   B. Jonny is regarded as a stand up guy, a responsible parent, and he doesn't give up until a task is finished.
   C. Each employee must submit a drug test each month.
   D. One of the documents was incinerated in the explosion.

   3.____

4.
   A. As soon as my parents get home, I told them I finished all of my chores.
   B. I asked my teacher to send me my missing work, check my absences, and how did I do on my test.
   C. Matt attempted to keep it concealed from Jenny and me.
   D. If Mary or him cannot get work done on time, I will have to split them up.

   4.____

5.
   A. Driving to work, the traffic report warned him of an accident on Highway 47.
   B. Jimmy has performed well this season.
   C. Since finishing her degree, several job offers have been given to Cam.
   D. Our boss is creating unstable conditions for we employees.

   5.____

6.
   A. The thief was described as a tall man with a wiry mustache weighing approximately 150 pounds.
   B. She gave Patrick and I some more time to finish our work.
   C. One of the books that he ordered was damaged in shipping.
   D. While talking on the rotary phone, the car Jim was driving skidded off the road.

   6.____

Questions 7-9.

DIRECTIONS: Questions 7 through 9 are to be answered on the basis of the following graph.

Ice Lake Frozen Flight (2002-2013)		
Year	Number of Participants	Temperature (Fahrenheit)
2002	22	4°
2003	50	33°
2004	69	18°
2005	104	22°
2006	108	24°
2007	288	33°
2008	173	9°
2009	598	39°
2010	698	26°
2011	696	30°
2012	777	28°
2013	578	32°

7. Which two year span had the LARGEST difference between temperatures? 7.____
   A. 2002 and 2003
   B. 2011 and 2012
   C. 2008 and 2009
   D. 2003 and 2004

8. How many total people participated in the years after the temperature reached at least 29°? 8.____
   A. 2,295   B. 1,717   C. 2,210   D. 4,543

9. In 2007, the event saw 288 participants, while in 2008 that number dropped to 173. Which of the following reasons BEST explains the drop in participants? 9.____
   A. The event had not been going on that long and people didn't know about it.
   B. The lake water wasn't cold enough to have people jump in.
   C. The temperature was too cold for many people who would have normally participated.
   D. None of the above reasons explain the drop in participants.

10. In the following list of numbers, how many times does 4 come just after 2 when 2 comes just after an odd number? 10.____
    2365247653898632488572486392424
    A. 2   B. 3   C. 4   D. 5

11. Which choice below lists the letter that is as far after B as S is after N in the alphabet? 11.____
    A. G   B. H   C. I   D. J

Questions 12-15.

DIRECTIONS: Questions 12 through 15 are to be answered on the basis of the following directory and list of changes.

Directory		
Name	Emp. Type	Position
Julie Taylor	Warehouse	Packer
James King	Office	Administrative Assistant
John Williams	Office	Salesperson
Ray Moore	Warehouse	Maintenance
Kathleen Byrne	Warehouse	Supervisor
Amy Jones	Office	Salesperson
Paul Jonas	Office	Salesperson
Lisa Wong	Warehouse	Loader
Eugene Lee	Office	Accountant
Bruce Lavine	Office	Manager
Adam Gates	Warehouse	Packer
Will Suter	Warehouse	Packer
Gary Lorper	Office	Accountant
Jon Adams	Office	Salesperson
Susannah Harper	Office	Salesperson

Directory Updates:
- Employee e-mail addresses will adhere to the following guidelines: lastnamefirstname@apexindustries.com (ex. Susannah Harper is harpersusannah@apexindustries.com). Currently, employees in the warehouse share one e-mail, distribution@apexindustries.com.
- The "Loader" position will now be referred to as "Specialist I"
- Adam Gates has accepted a Supervisor position within the Warehouse and is no longer a Packer. All warehouse employees report to the two Supervisors and all office employees report to the Manager.

12. Amy Jones tried to send an e-mail to Adam Gates, but it wouldn't send. 12.____
    Which of the following offers the BEST explanation?
    A. Amy put Adam's first name first and then his last name.
    B. Adam doesn't check his e-mail, so he wouldn't know if he received the e-mail or not.
    C. Adam does not have his own e-mail.
    D. Office employees are not allowed to send e-mails to each other.

13. How many Packers currently work for Apex Industries? 13.____
    A. 2   B. 3   C. 4   D. 5

14. What position does Lisa Wong currently hold? 14.____
    A. Specialist I   B. Secretary
    C. Administrative Assistant   D. Loader

15. If an employee wanted to contact the office manager, which of the following e-mails should the e-mail be sent to? 15.____
    A. officemanager@apexindustries.com
    B. brucelavine@apexindustries.com
    C. lavinebruce@apexindustries.com
    D. distribution@apexindustries.com

Questions 16-19.

DIRECTIONS: In answering Questions 16 through 19, compare the three names, numbers or addresses.

16. Smiley Yarnell   Smiley Yarnel   Smily Yarnell   16.____
    A. All three are exactly alike.
    B. The first and second are exactly alike.
    C. The second and third are exactly alike.
    D. All three are different.

17. 1583 Theater Drive   1583 Theater Drive   1583 Theatre Drive   17.____
    A. All three are exactly alike.
    B. The first and second are exactly alike.
    C. The second and third are exactly alike.
    D. All three are different.

18. 3341893212   3341893212   3341893212   18.____
    A. All three are exactly alike.
    B. The first and second are exactly alike.
    C. The second and third are exactly alike.
    D. All three are different.

19. Douglass Watkins   Douglas Watkins   Douglass Watkins   19.____
    A. All three are exactly alike.
    B. The first and third are exactly alike.
    C. The second and third are exactly alike.
    D. All three are different.

Questions 20-24.

DIRECTIONS: In answering Questions 20 through 24, you will be presented with a word. Choose the synonym that BEST represents the word in question.

20. Flexible   20.____
    A. delicate   B. inflammable   C. strong   D. pliable

21. Alternative   21.____
    A. choice   B. moderate   C. lazy   D. value

22. Corroborate
    A. examine   B. explain   C. verify   D. explain   22.____

23. Respiration
    A. recovery   B. breathing   C. sweating   D. selfish   23.____

24. Negligent
    A. lazy   B. moderate   C. hopeless   D. lax   24.____

25. Plumber is to Wrench as Painter is to   25.____
    A. pipe   B. shop   C. hammer   D. brush

KEY (CORRECT ANSWERS)

1.	D		11.	A
2.	A		12.	C
3.	D		13.	A
4.	C		14.	A
5.	B		15.	C
6.	C		16.	D
7.	C		17.	B
8.	B		18.	A
9.	C		19.	B
10.	C		20.	D

21. A
22. C
23. B
24. D
25. D

FILING

EXAMINATION SECTION
TEST 1

DIRECTIONS: For each of the following, you are given a name above and three other names in alphabetical order below. The letters A, B, C, and D stand for spaces where you could file the name. Find the CORRECT space for the name given above so that it will be in alphabetical order with the names below it. The letter that stands for that space is the answer to the question.

1. CURRAN, THOMAS
   A CURLEY, MARY B CURR, SAMUEL C CURREN, KATIE D

2. KAPLIN, EDWIN
   A KAPLEN, MICHAEL B KAPLIN, JULIA C KAPLON, DAVID D

3. PENSKY, LEONA
   A PENSLER, SANDY B PENSLEY, JOEL C PENSLEY, JOSEPH D

4. ROWEN, MARCIA
   A ROWEN, CHRISTOPHER B ROWEN, LOUIS C ROWEN, MARTIN D

5. FOSTER, GRACE
   A FOSS, EARL B FOSSE, NICHOLE C FOSTER, KEITH D

6. KO, FAI
   A KO, HOK B KO, HUNG-FAI C KO, HYUN JUNG D

7. MICHALIK, ANTHONY
   A MICHALIC, GARY B MICHALIS, HELEN C MICHALK, KLAUS D

8. MINTZ, JUDITH
   A MINTZ, JAKE B MINTZ, JAMES C MINTZ, JULIUS D

9. POWERS, ANN
   A POUST, THERESE B POWELL, LUTHER C POWER, RACHEL D

10. PRACTICAL STUDIO, INC.
    A PRACTICAL PUBLISHING B PRACTICE DEVELOPMENT C PRACTICE SERVICE CORP. D

11. SHERWIN, ROBERTA
    A SHERWIN, RAUL B SHERWIN, RICHARD C SHERWIN, ROBERT D

12. JACOBSEN, JENNIFER
    A JACOBSON, PETER B JACOBY, JACK C JACOVITZ, GAIL D

13. BLEINHEIM, GLORIA
    A BLELOCK, JULIA B BLENCOWE, FRED C BLENMAN, ANTHONY D

14. FIRST STERLING CORP. 14.____
    A̲ FIRST STATE PRODUCTS B̲ FIRST STEP INC. C̲ FIRST STOP CORP. D̲

15. VICKERS, GEORGE 15.____
    A̲ VICHEY, LOUIS B̲ VICHI, MARIO C̲ VICKI, SUSAN D̲

16. STEIN, DAVID 16.____
    A̲ STEIN, CRAIG B̲ STEIN, DANIEL C̲ STEIN, DEBORAH D̲

17. IGLESIAS, BERNADETTE 17.____
    A̲ IGER, MARTIN B̲ IGLEHEART, PHYLICIA C̲ IGLEWSKI, RICHARD D̲

18. IDEAL ROOFING CORP. 18.____
    A̲ IDEAL REPRODUCTION B̲ IDEAL RESTAURANT C̲ IDEAL RUBBER PRODUCTS D̲

19. TODARO, JOSEPH 19.____
    A̲ TODD, ANNE B̲ TODE, WALLY C̲ TODMAN, JUDITH D̲

20. WILKERSON, RUTH 20.____
    A̲ WILKENS, FRANK B̲ WILKES, BARRY C̲ WILKIE, JANE D̲

21. HUGHES, MARY 21.____
    A̲ HUGHES, MANUEL B̲ HUGHES, MARGARET C̲ HUGHES, MARTHA D̲

22. GODWIN, JAMES 22.____
    A̲ GODFREY, SONDRA B̲ GODMAN, GABRIEL C̲ GODREAU, ROBERT D̲

23. NACHMAN, DAVID 23.____
    A̲ NACHT, JAMES B̲ NACK, SAUL C̲ NACKENSON, LORI D̲

24. CASPER, LAURENCE 24.____
    A̲ CASPER, LEONARD B̲ CASPER, LESTER C̲ CASPER, LINDA D̲

25. CULEN, ELLEN 25.____
    A̲ CULHANE, JOHN B̲ CULICHI, RADU C̲ CULIN, TERRY D̲

KEY (CORRECT ANSWERS)

1.	C	11.	D
2.	B	12.	A
3.	A	13.	A
4.	C	14.	C
5.	C	15.	C
6.	A	16.	C
7.	B	17.	C
8.	C	18.	C
9.	D	19.	A
10.	B	20.	B

21. D
22. D
23. A
24. A
25. A

TEST 2

DIRECTIONS: For each of the following, you are given a name above and three other names in alphabetical order below. The letters A, B, C, and D stand for spaces where you could file the name. Find the CORRECT space for the name given above so that it will be in alphabetical order with the names below it. The letter that stands for that space is the answer to the question.

1. HARMAN, HENRY
   A HARLEY, LILLIAN B HARMER, RALPH C HARMON, CECIL D

2. MANNING, JOHNSON
   A MANNING, JAMES B MANNING, JEROME C MANNING, JOHN D

3. NOGUCHI, JANICE
   A NOEL, WALTER B NOGUET, DANIELLE C NOH, DAVID D

4. PARRON, ALFONSE
   A PARRIS, LEON B PARRISH, LINDA C PARROTT, BETTY D

5. GROSS, ELANA
   A GROSS, ELAINE B GROSS, ELIZABETH C GROSS, ELLIOT D

6. HORSTMANN, ANNA
   A HORSMAN, ALLAN B HORST, VALERIE C HORSTMAN, JAMES D

7. JONES, EMILY
   A JONES, ELMA B JONES, ELOISE C JONES, EMMA D

8. LESSING, FRED
   A LESSER, MARTHA B LESSIN, ELLIE C LESSNER, ERWIN D

9. ROSENBLUM, JULIUS
   A ROSENBLUTH, SYLVIA B ROSENBORG, ERIC C ROSENBURG, JANE D

10. YOUNG, THEODORE
    A YOUNG, TERRY B YOUNG, THELMA C YOUNG, THOMAS D

11. RENICK, KAREN
    A RENIE, JOSEPH B RENITA, JOSE C RENKO, DORIS D

12. ADLER, HELEN
    A ADLER, HAROLD B ADLER, HARRY C ADLER, HENRY D

13. BURKHARDT, ANN
    A BURKET, HARRIET B BURKHOLDER, CARL C BURKHOLZ, SCOTT D

14. DE LUCA, PAUL
    A DE LUCA, JOHN B DE LUCIA, AUDREY C DE LUCIA, ROBERT D

15. DEMBSKI, STEPHEN
    A DEMBLING, JOAN B DEMBNER, PETER C DEMBROW, HELEN D

16. FLYNN, ARCHIE 16.____
    A FLYNN, AGNES B FLYNN, ANDREW C FLYNN, ANNMARIE D

17. GRAFFY, PAUL 17.____
    A GRAFMAN, ANDREW B GRAFSTEIN, BETTY C GRAFTON, MELVIN D

18. KERMIT, FRANK 18.____
    A KERMAN, LINDA B KERMISH, RHODA C KERMOYAN, MICKI D

19. METZLER, MAURICE 19.____
    A METZGER, ALFRED B METZIER, SONIA C METZINGER, PAUL D

20. PADDINGTON, TIMOTHY 20.____
    A PADDEN, MICHAEL B PADDISON, BRUCE C PADELL, EUNICE D

21. RICHARDSON, BLANCHE 21.____
    A RICHARDSON, BETTY B RICHARDSON, BEVERLY C RICHARDSON, BRENDA D

22. ISEKI, EMILE 22.____
    A ISELIN, CAROL B ISEN, RICHARD C ISENEE, CYNTHIA D

23. CONNELL, EUGENE 23.____
    A CONNELL, EDWARD B CONNELL, HELEN C CONNELL, HUGH D

24. MAC LEOD, LAURIE 24.____
    A MAC LEOD, LORNA B MC LANE, PAUL C MC LAREN, DUNCAN D

25. BOLE, KENNETH 25.____
    A BOLDEN, ROSIE B BOLDT, LINDA C BOLELLA, DENNIS D

KEY (CORRECT ANSWERS)

1.	B		11.	A
2.	D		12.	C
3.	B		13.	B
4.	C		14.	B
5.	B		15.	D
6.	D		16.	D
7.	C		17.	A
8.	C		18.	C
9.	A		19.	D
10.	C		20.	B

21. C
22. A
23. B
24. A
25. C

TEST 3

DIRECTIONS: For each of the following, you are given a name above and three other names in alphabetical order below. The letters A, B, C, and D stand for spaces where you could file the name. Find the CORRECT space for the name given above so that it will be in alphabetical order with the names below it. The letter that stands for that space is the answer to the question.

1. CARLISLE, ALAN
   A CARLINSKY, LEONA B CARLITOS, JUAN C CARLL, CHARLES D
   1.____

2. COLLINS, KAREN
   A COLLINS, KATHLEEN B COLLINS, KATHRYN C COLLINS, KAY D
   2.____

3. GALLOTTI, OSCAR
   A GALLONTY, FRANCIS B GALLOP, LILLIAN C GALLOU, ALEXIS D
   3.____

4. MAHADY, JOHN
   A MAHADEO, PRATAB B MAHAJAN, ASHA C MAHARAJAH, MIARIAM D
   4.____

5. WINGATE, REBECCA
   A WINGARD, LUCILLE B WINGAT, ROBERT C WINGER, HOLLY D
   5.____

6. ZWEIGHAFT, FREDA
   A ZWEIG, BERTRAM B ZWEIGBAUM, BENJAMIN C ZWEIGENTHAL, DOROTHY D
   6.____

7. MAXWELL, GEORGE
   A MAXWELL, EDWARD B MAXWELL, FRANK C MAXWELL, HARRIS D
   7.____

8. O'DOHERTY, SALLY
   A ODETTE, CHARLES B ODIOTTI, MASSIE C ODNORALOV, MIKHAEL D
   8.____

9. JAMES, ROGER
   A JAMIESON, KELLY B JAMNER, ELIZABETH C JAMPOLSKY, MILTON D
   9.____

10. PADIN, FRANCIS
    A PADILLA, ANGELA B PADINGER, JENNY C PADLEY, RAYMOND D
    10.____

11. AAARMAN, ALEC
    A AABY, JANE B AACH, ALBERT C AACHEN, HENRY D
    11.____

12. BILLHARDT, PHILIP
    A BILLERA, FRANKLIN B BILLIG, LESLIE C BILLINGS, CAROL D
    12.____

13. LADEROS, ELANA
    A LADENHEIM, HELENE B LADERMAN, SAM C LADHA, SANDRA D
    13.____

14. PUCKERING, DENNIS
    A PUCKETT, AUDREY B PUCKNAT, JOHN C PUCKO, BENNY D
    14.____

15. SCHOLZE, GEORGE
    A SCHOLNICK, LEONARD B SCHOLOSS, JACK C SCHOLZ, PAUL D
    15.____

16. WILSON, MERYL   16.____
    A WILSON, MERIMAN B WILSON, MERRY C WILSON, MERRYL D

17. ZUKOWSKI, MICHAEL   17.____
    A ZWACK, ALEXA B ZYKO, KATHERINE C ZYMAN, HERBERT D

18. MC CANNA, THOMAS   18.____
    A MC CANN, GERALD B MC CANNA, JANET C MC CANTS, MOLLIE D

19. PHILIPP, SUSANE   19.____
    A PHILIP, PETER B PHILIPOSE, ANDREW C PHILIPPE, BEATRICE D

20. KINGPIN, PAUL   20.____
    A KINGDON, KENNETH B KINGMAN, JEAN C KINGOLD, RICHARD D

21. HAMILTON, DONALD   21.____
    A HAMILTON, DON B HAMILTON, DOROTHY C HAMILTON, DOUGLAS D

22. BAEL, ELAINE   22.____
    A BAELE, GUSTAVE B BAEN, JAMES C BAENA, ARIEL D

23. BILL, KASEY   23.____
    A BILGINER, NATHAN B BILKAY, WILLIAM C BILLES, BRADFORD D

24. CARLEN, ELLIOT   24.____
    A CARINO, NAN B CARLE, JOHN C CARLESI, ANTHONY D

25. LOURIE, DONALD   25.____
    A LOUIE, ROSE B LOUIS, STEVE C LOVE, MARCIA D

KEY (CORRECT ANSWERS)

1.	B	11.	A
2.	A	12.	B
3.	C	13.	C
4.	B	14.	A
5.	C	15.	D
6.	D	16.	D
7.	C	17.	A
8.	D	18.	C
9.	A	19.	C
10.	B	20.	D

21. B
22. A
23. C
24. C
25. C

TEST 4

DIRECTIONS: For each of the following, you are given a name above and three other names in alphabetical order below. The letters A, B, C, and D stand for spaces where you could file the name. Find the CORRECT space for the name given above so that it will be in alphabetical order with the names below it. The letter that stands for that space is the answer to the question.

1. DEMOPOULOS, GUS
   A DEMOPOULOS, DIMITRI B DEMOPOULOS, HELEN C DEMOPOULOS, LAURA D

   1.____

2. DRUMWRIGHT, BRUCE
   A DRUMMOND, RANDY B DRUMMUND, WALTER C DRUMRIGHT, JULIUS D

   2.____

3. GRAHAM, LETICIA
   A GRAHAM, LEON B GRAHAM, LEROY C GRAHAM, LESLIE D

   3.____

4. KELLEHER, KEVIN
   A KELLARD, WILLIAM B KELLEDY, JAMES C KELLEHER, KRISTINE D

   4.____

5. LIANG, JAN
   A LIANG, JIE B LIANG, JIN CHANG C LIANG, JIN HE D

   5.____

6. MOLINELLI, STEVE
   A MOLINAR, RICARDO B MOLINER, LOUISA C MOLINI, OSCAR D

   6.____

7. PARRILLA, EMANUEL
   A PARRAS, TONY B PARRETTA, JOSEPHINE C PARRETTA, NANCY D

   7.____

8. SILBERFARD, MILDRED
   A SILBERBERG, SEYMOUR B SILBERBLATT, JOHN C SILBERFARB, SYLVIA D

   8.____

9. TOLANI, ROHET
   A TOLAN, DOROTHY B TOLASSI, JOANNA C TOLBERT, ALICE D

   9.____

10. VIERA, DIANE
    A VIERA, DIANA B VIERA, ELLIOT C VIERA, JAMES D

    10.____

11. KLAUER, MICHAEL
    A KLAUBER, ALFRED B KLAUBERG, SUSAN C KLAUS, MARJORIE D

    11.____

12. REEVES, MARIE
    A REEVES, MATTHEW B REEVES, MELVIN C REEVES, ORALEE D

    12.____

13. DEL VALLE, JULIA
    A DEL VALLE, EMMA B DEL VALLE, GLORIA C DEL VALLE, JOSEPH D

    13.____

14. LAIO, SHU-YU
    A LAING, VINCENT B LAIRO, SCOTT C LAIS, STEVE D

    14.____

15. MENDEZ, ROBERTO
    A MENDELSON, SOL B MENDES, MAE C MENDOZA, HUGO D

    15.____

16. ALBRIGHT, LEE 16.____
    <u>A</u> ALBRACHT, MARIE <u>B</u> ALBRECHT, VICTOR <u>C</u> ALBRINK, JOAN <u>D</u>

17. CAIN, STEPHEN 17.____
    <u>A</u> CAIN, SAMUEL <u>B</u> CAIN, SHARON <u>C</u> CAIN, SIBOL <u>D</u>

18. HOPKOWITZ, THOMAS 18.____
    <u>A</u> HOPKINS, CYNTHIA <u>B</u> HOPPENFELD, DENIS <u>C</u> HOPPER, ELSA <u>D</u>

19. LUMBLY, KAREN 19.____
    <u>A</u> LUMBI, JENNY <u>B</u> LUME, JIMMIE <u>C</u> LUMEN, GAIL <u>D</u>

20. MAYER, MORTON 20.____
    <u>A</u> MAYER, MONROE <u>B</u> MAYER, MORRIS <u>C</u> MAYER, MYRON <u>D</u>

21. YOUNGER, LORRAINE 21.____
    <u>A</u> YOUNGHEM, THEODORE <u>B</u> YOUNGMAN, LEIF <u>C</u> YOUNGS, FRED <u>D</u>

22. THORSEN, HILDA 22.____
    <u>A</u> THORNWELL, PERCY <u>B</u> THORON, LLOYD <u>C</u> THORP, JACQUELINE <u>D</u>

23. MC DERMOTT, BETTY 23.____
    <u>A</u> MC DEARMON, WILLIAM <u>B</u> MC DEVITT, BERYL <u>C</u> MC DONAGH, DANIEL <u>D</u>

24. BLUMENTHAL, SIMON 24.____
    <u>A</u> BLUMENTHAL, SHIRLEY <u>B</u> BLUMENTHAL, SIDNEY <u>C</u> BLUMENTHAL, SOLOMON <u>D</u>

25. ERVINS, RICHARD 25.____
    <u>A</u> ERVIN, BERTHA <u>B</u> ERVING, THELMA <u>C</u> ERWIN, EUGENE <u>D</u>

KEY (CORRECT ANSWERS)

1. B
2. D
3. D
4. C
5. A

6. B
7. D
8. D
9. B
10. B

11. C
12. A
13. D
14. B
15. C

16. C
17. D
18. B
19. B
20. C

21. A
22. D
23. B
24. C
25. C

TEST 5

DIRECTIONS: For each of the following, you are given a name above and three other names in alphabetical order below. The letters A, B, C, and D stand for spaces where you could file the name. Find the CORRECT space for the name given above so that it will be in alphabetical order with the names below it. The letter that stands for that space is the answer to the question.

1. GUIDRY, THELMA
   A GUIDONE, GEORGE B GUIGLI, PAMELA C GUIGNON, DANIEL D

   1.____

2. JAMES, ALLAN
   A JAMES, ALMA B JAMES, AMY C JAMES, ANNA D

   2.____

3. LESSOFF, CONNIE
   A LESSIK, JAKE B LESSING, LEONARD C LESSNER, ADELE D

   3.____

4. MONTNER, LUIS
   A MONTEFIORE, ANDREW B MONTILLA, IRIS C MONTINI, ALEXANDRA D

   4.____

5. PHELPS, KENNETH
   A PHELEN, JAMES B PHELON, RANDY C PHETT, GARY D

   5.____

6. STAVSKY, STANLEY
   A STAVROS, MIKE B STAWSKI, LILLIAN C STAWSKI, NAOMI D

   6.____

7. GROSSMAN, WILL
   A GROSSMAN, WENDY B GROSSMANN, WAYNE C GROSSMANN, WILLA D

   7.____

8. IRES, JEFFREY
   A IRENA, THOMAS B IRENE, JAY C IRES, HOWARD D

   8.____

9. NIKOLAOU, CHRISTINE
   A NIKOLAIS, GERRARD B NIKOLAKAKOS, GEORGE C NIKOLATOS, HARRY D

   9.____

10. TURCO, KEITH
    A TURCHIN, DEBORAH B TURCI, GINA C TURCK, KATHRYN D

    10.____

11. WORLEY, DIANE
    A WORMAN, STELLA B WORMER, SARA C WORMLEY, ROBERT D

    11.____

12. DRUSIN, GUY
    A DRURY, JESSICA B DRUSE, KEN C DRUSS, THERESA D

    12.____

13. LYONS, JAMES
    A LYONS, ERNST B LYONS, INGRID C LYONS, KEVIN D

    13.____

14. NOBLE, BERNARD
    A NOBEL, LOUISE B NOBILE, DENNIS C NOBIS, JAMES D

    14.____

15. O'DELL, ERIN
    A O'DAY, PATRICIA B O'DEA, MAUREEN C O'DELL, GWYNN D

    15.____

16. POUPON, LOUIS
    A POULSON, SIMON B POURE, DAMIAN C POURIDAS, CARMEN D

    16._____

17. REMEY, NAOMI
    A REMES, STUART B REMEZ, ALFREDO C REMIEN, ROBERT D

    17._____

18. WATSON, LAURENCE
    A WATSON, LENORA B WATSON, LEONARD C WATSON, LLOYD D

    18._____

19. AMSILI, MORTON
    A AMSDEN, ESTHER B AMSEL, HYMAN C ARES, MEYER D

    19._____

20. CLEMMONS, BERTHA
    A CLEMENT, GILBERT B CLEMINSON, DEAN C CLEMONS, GLADYS D

    20._____

21. LAMPERT, EDNA
    A LAMPIER, JANICE B LAMPKIN, ALYCE C LAMPKOWSKI, DENNIS D

    21._____

22. LIBERTO, DON
    A LIBERMAN, MATTIE B LIBERSON, MIRIAM C LIBERTY, ARTHUR D

    22._____

23. REVENZON, ISABELLA
    A REVELEY, RUTH B REVELLE, GRACE C REVERE, EDITH D

    23._____

24. BURKHALTER, HAZEL
    A BURKE, WINSTON B BURKETT, BENJAMIN C BURKEY, WAYNE D

    24._____

25. DORSEY, HAROLD
    A DOSHER, EILEEN B DOSHIRE, BURTON C DOSSIL, RICHARD D

    25._____

KEY (CORRECT ANSWERS)

1.	B	11.	A
2.	A	12.	C
3.	D	13.	C
4.	D	14.	D
5.	C	15.	C
6.	B	16.	B
7.	B	17.	B
8.	D	18.	A
9.	C	19.	C
10.	D	20.	C

21. A
22. C
23. C
24. D
25. A

TEST 6

DIRECTIONS: For each of the following, you are given a name above and three other names in alphabetical order below. The letters A, B, C, and D stand for spaces where you could file the name. Find the CORRECT space for the name given above so that it will be in alphabetical order with the names below it. The letter that stands for that space is the answer to the question.

1. HATFIELD, NICOLA
   A HATCHER, JOHN B HATELY, BRIAN C HATGIS, ELLEN D

2. IVANOFF, HELENA
   A IVAN, LEONARD B IVANOV, SERGE C IVANY, EMERY D

3. KELKER, NORMAN
   A KELFER, STEPHANE B KELING, JAY C KELISON, ABE D

4. ROGGENBURG, LEE
   A ROGERS, SHARON B ROGET, ALLAN C ROGGERO, MORGAN D

5. SMITH, ALENA
   A SMITH, AARON B SMITH, AGNES C SMITH, ALBERT D

6. ZOLOR, RONALD
   A ZOLNAK, SUSANNA B ZOLOTH, SAMUEL C ZOLOTO, PEARL D

7. ERRICH, GRETCHEN
   A ERREICH, RENE B ERRERA, STEVEN C ERRETT, ALICE D

8. CARDWELL, MELASAN
   A CARDUCCI, RONALD B CARDULLO, MIKE C CARDY, FREDRIK D

9. MOFFAT, SARAH
   A MOFFET, JONATHAN B MOFFIE, LISA C MOFFITT, LAUREN D

10. PARRINO, WAYNE
    A PARRETTA, MICHELE B PARRILLA, BERNIE C PARRINELLO, CARRIE D

11. PINSLEY, SETH
    A PINSKY, GLORIA B PINSON, BENNET C PINTADO, MARIE D

12. FREEMAN, ELMIRA
    A FREEMAN, EDITH B FREEMAN, ERIC C FREEMAN, ETHEL D

13. BERLINGER, SOPHIE
    A BERLEY, DAVID B BERLIND, ARNOLD C BERLINGER, FREDA D

14. ANIELLO, JOSEPH
    A ANGULO, ADOLFO B ANHALT, LINDA C ANIBAL, VINCENT D

15. LACHER, LEO
    A LACHET, MARGARET B LACHINI, KAY C LACHIVER, ANDREA D

16. ROBINSON, MARION   16.___
    A ROBINSON, MARCIA B ROBINSON, MARGARET C ROBINSON, MARIETTA D

17. ULRICH, DENNIS   17.___
    A ULMAN, CANDY B ULMER, TED C ULRIED, RICHARD D

18. ASHINSKY, ROSS   18.___
    A ASHKAR, MICHAEL B ASHKE, PAUL C ASHKIN, ROBERTA D

19. LITVAK, DARRELL   19.___
    A LITUCHY, BEVERLY B LITVIN, SAM C LITWACK, MARTIN D

20. SLATTERY, GERALD   20.___
    A SLATER, NELLIE B SLATKIN, HEIDI C SLATKY, IRVING D

21. MCCANTS, GEORGIA   21.___
    A MCCANN, CHERYL B MCCANNA, THOMAS C MCCARDELL, GARY D

22. HARMER, AVA   22.___
    A HARLOW, JULES B HARLSON, NORMAN C HARMEL, SHARON D

23. CALDERONE, PHILIP   23.___
    A CALDERIN, ANA B CALDON, WALTER C CALDRON, MICHELE D

24. GINSBURG, ISAAC   24.___
    A GINSBURG, EDWARD B GINSBURG, GERALD C GINSBURG, HILDA D

25. LEE, LEIGH   25.___
    A LEE, LELA B LEE, LELAND C LEE, LEON D

KEY (CORRECT ANSWERS)

1.	C		11.	B
2.	B		12.	B
3.	D		13.	D
4.	C		14.	D
5.	D		15.	A
6.	B		16.	D
7.	D		17.	C
8.	C		18.	A
9.	A		19.	B
10.	D		20.	D

21. C
22. D
23. B
24. D
25. A

TEST 7

DIRECTIONS: For each of the following, you are given a name above and three other names in alphabetical order below. The letters A, B, C, and D stand for spaces where you could file the name. Find the CORRECT space for the name given above so that it will be in alphabetical order with the names below it. The letter that stands for that space is the answer to the question.

1. POWERS, PHYLLIS
   A POWELL, HATTIE B POWER, EDWARD C POWLETT, WENDY D   1._____

2. SILVERA, IRWIN
   A SILVA, ANGEL B SILVANO, FRANK C SILVERIA, ANNA D   2._____

3. BACHRACH, DAN
   A BACHMANN, DONNA B BACHNER, LESTER C BACHOWSKI, JEWEL D   3._____

4. RIVERA, RAMON
   A RIVAS, ERICA B RIVES, SHARON C RIVIER, CLAUDE D   4._____

5. WEINSTOCK, JEFFREY
   A WEINSTEIN, PAUL B WEINSTONE, ALAN C WEINTRAUB, MARCI D   5._____

6. AMANDA, STEPHAN
   A AMADO, DANIELLO B AMALIA, JOSE C AMAR, LISA D   6._____

7. HERRON, LOUIS
   A HERSCH, JACK B HERSCHELL, GREGORY C HERSCHER, GAIL D   7._____

8. REEDY, ARTHUR
   A REED, ALEX B REESE, JOHN C REEVE, DAVE D   8._____

9. FLORIN, RAYMOND
   A FLORENTINO, PAULA B FLORES, MITCHEL C FLORIAN, CARLO D   9._____

10. HOROWITZ, ELLIOT
    A HOROWITZ, FRANKLIN B HOROWITZ, IRA C HOROWITZ, JOAN D   10._____

11. KNOPFLER, WOODY
    A KNOBLER, HENRY B KNOLL, GEORGE C KNOPF, LAURA D   11._____

12. OTIN, JENNIFER
    A OTERO, ALBERT B OTHON, DOROTHY C OTIS, JAMES D   12._____

13. SACHA, IRENE
    A SACCO, HEATHER B SACHNER, JULIE C SACHS, DAVID D   13._____

14. WORTHY, PRISCILLA
    A WORTH, ROBERT B WORTHINGTON, SUSAN C WORTMAN, MYRA D   14._____

15. ZUCKERMAN, GARY
    A ZUKER, JEROME B ZUKOWSKI, CHRIS C ZULACK, JOHN D   15._____

2 (#7)

16. BRIEGER, CLARENCE 16.____
    A BRIEF, SIGMUND B BRIELLE, JEAN C BRIELOFF, SAUL D

17. FOSTER, AGNES 17.____
    A FOSTER, ADDIE B FOSTER, ALBERT C FOSTER, ALICE D

18. LIBERSTEIN, MIRIAM 18.____
    A LIBERMAN, HERMAN B LIBERSON, RUBIN C LIBERT, NAT D

19. PRICKETT, DELORES 19.____
    A PRICE, WILLIAM B PRICHARD, STEPHANY C PRITCHETT, KENNETH D

20. TRIBBLE, RITA 20.____
    A TRIAS, JOSE B TRIBBIT, CHARLES C TRIBE, SIENNA D

21. ZOBEL, MAX 21.____
    A ZOBACK, DERRICK B ZOBALI, KIERSTAN C ZOBERG, STUART D

22. HOTRA, WALTER 22.____
    A HOTT, NELL B HOTTENSEN, ROBERT C HOTTON, BRUCE D

23. MICHELL, CARL 23.____
    A MICHELE, KAREN B MICHELMAN, BERTHA C MICHELS, GLORIA D

24. RAFFERTY, GEORGE 24.____
    A RAFFERTY, HAROLD B RAFFERTY, KEVIN C RAFFERTY, LUCILLE D

25. OLIVIERI, ALLAN 25.____
    A OLIVIERO, FRANK B OLIVRY, RAUL C OLIZEIRA, CHARLES D

KEY (CORRECT ANSWERS)

1. C
2. C
3. D
4. B
5. B

6. C
7. A
8. B
9. D
10. A

11. D
12. C
13. B
14. C
15. A

16. B
17. B
18. C
19. C
20. C

21. C
22. A
23. B
24. A
25. A

ARITHMETICAL REASONING
EXAMINATION SECTION
TEST 1

DIRECTIONS: Each question or incomplete statement is followed by several suggested answers or completions. Select the one that BEST answers the question or completes the statement. *PRINT THE LETTER OF THE CORRECT ANSWER IN THE SPACE AT THE RIGHT.*

1. If a secretary answered 28 phone calls and typed the addresses for 112 credit statements in one morning, what is the RATIO of phone calls answered to credit statements typed for that period of time?

    A. 1:4 B. 1:7 C. 2:3 D. 3:5

2. According to a suggested filing system, no more than 10 folders should be filed behind any one file guide and from 15 to 25 file guides should be used in each file drawer for easy finding and filing.
The MAXIMUM number of folders that a five-drawer file cabinet can hold to allow easy finding and filing is

    A. 550 B. 750 C. 1,100 D. 1,250

3. An employee had a starting salary of $19,353. He received a salary increase at the end of each year, and at the end of the seventh year his salary was $25,107.
What was his AVERAGE annual increase in salary over these seven years?

    A. $765 B. $807 C. $822 D. $858

4. The 55 typists and 28 senior clerks in a certain agency were paid a total of $1,457,400 in salaries in 2005.
If the average annual salary of a typist was $16,800, the average annual salary of a senior clerk was

    A. $19,050 B. $19,950 C. $20,100 D. $20,250

5. A typist has been given a three-page report to type. She has finished typing the first two pages. The first page has 283 words, and the second page has 366 words.
If the total report consists of 954 words, how many words will she have to type on the third page of the report?

    A. 202 B. 287 C. 305 D. 313

6. In one day, Clerk A processed 30% more forms than Clerk B, and Clerk C processed 1 1/4 as many forms as Clerk A.
If Clerk B processed 40 forms, how many more forms were processed by Clerk C than Clerk B?

    A. 12 B. 13 C. 21 D. 25

7. A clerk who earns a gross salary of $678 every 2 weeks has the following deductions taken from her paycheck: 15% for city, state, and federal taxes; 2 1/2% for Social Security; $1.95 for health insurance; and $9.00 for union dues.
The amount of her take-home pay is

   A. $429.60   B. $468.60   C. $497.40   D. $548.40

8. In 2002, an agency spent $400 to buy pencils at a cost of $1.00 a dozen.
If the agency used 3/4 of these pencils in 2002 and used the same number of pencils in 2003, how many more pencils did it have to buy to have enough pencils for all of 2003?

   A. 1,200   B. 2,400   C. 3,600   D. 4,800

9. A clerk who worked in Agency X earned the following salaries: $15,105 the first year, $15,750 the second year, and $16,440 the third year. Another clerk who worked in Agency Y for three years earned $15,825 a year for two years and $16,086 the third year. The DIFFERENCE between the average salaries received by both clerks over a three-year period is

   A. $147   B. $153   C. $261   D. $423

10. An employee who works more than 40 hours in any week receives overtime payment for the extra hours at time and one-half (1 1/2 times) his hourly rate of pay. An employee who earns $13.60 an hour works a total of 45 hours during a certain week.
His TOTAL pay for that week would be

    A. $564.40   B. $612.00   C. $646.00   D. $824.00

11. Suppose that the amount of money spent for supplies in 2006 for a division in a city department was $156,500. This represented an increase of 12% over the amount spent for supplies for this division in 2005.
The amount of money spent for supplies for this division in 2005 was MOST NEARLY

    A. $139,730   B. $137,720   C. $143,460   D. $138,720

12. Suppose that a group of five clerks have been assigned to insert 24,000 letters into envelopes. The clerks perform this work at the following rates of speed: Clerk A, 1,100 letters an hour; Clerk B, 1,450 letters an hour; Clerk C, 1,200 letters an hour; Clerk D, 1,300 letters an hour; Clerk E, 1,250 letters an hour. At the end of two hours of work, Clerks C and D are assigned to another task.
From the time that Clerks C and D were taken off the assignment, the number of hours required for the remaining clerks to complete this assignment is

    A. less than 3 hours
    B. 3 hours
    C. more than 3 hours, but less than 4 hours
    D. more than 4 hours

13. The number 60 is 40% of

    A. 24   B. 84   C. 96   D. 150

14. If 3/8 of a number is 96, the number is

    A. 132   B. 36   C. 256   D. 156

15. A city department uses an average of 25 20-cent, 35 30-cent, and 350 40-cent postage stamps each day.
    The TOTAL cost of stamps used by the department in a five-day period is

    A. $29.50   B. $155.50   C. $290.50   D. $777.50

16. A city department issued 12,000 applications in 2000. The number of applications that the department issued in 1998 was 25% greater than the number it issued in 2000.
    If the department issued 10% fewer applications in 1996 than it did in 1998, the number it issued in 1996 was

    A. 16,500   B. 13,500   C. 9,900   D. 8,100

17. A clerk can add 40 columns of figures an hour by using an adding machine and 20 columns of figures an hour without using an adding machine.
    The TOTAL number of hours it would take him to add 200 columns if he does 3/5 of the work by machine and the rest without the machine is

    A. 6   B. 7   C. 8   D. 9

18. In 1997, a city department bought 500 dozen pencils at $1.20 per dozen. In 2000, only 75 percent as many pencils were bought as were bought in 1997, but the price was 20 percent higher than the 1997 price. The TOTAL cost of the pencils bought in 2000 was

    A. $540   B. $562.50   C. $720   D. $750

19. A clerk is assigned to check the accuracy of the entries on 490 forms. He checks 40 forms an hour. After working one hour on this task, he is joined by another clerk, who checks these forms at the rate of 35 an hour.
    The TOTAL number of hours required to do the entire assignment is

    A. 5   B. 6   C. 7   D. 8

20. Assume that there are a total of 420 employees in a city agency. Thirty percent of the employees are clerks, and 1/7 are typists.
    The DIFFERENCE between the number of clerks and the number of typists is

    A. 126   B. 66   C. 186   D. 80

21. Assume that a duplicating machine produces copies of a bulletin at a cost of 2 cents per copy. The machine produces 120 copies of the bulletin per minute.
    If the cost of producing a certain number of copies was $12, how many minutes of operation did it take the machine to produce this number of copies?

    A. 5   B. 2   C. 10   D. 6

22. An assignment is completed by 32 clerks in 22 days. Assuming that all the clerks work at the same rate of speed, the number of clerks that would be needed to complete this assignment in 16 days is

    A. 27   B. 38   C. 44   D. 52

23. A department head hired a total of 60 temporary employees to handle a seasonal increase in the department's workload. The following lists the number of temporary employees hired, their rates of pay, and the duration of their employment:
   One-third of the total were hired as clerks, each at the rate of $27,500 a year, for two months.
   30 percent of the total were hired as office machine operators, each at the rate of $31,500 a year, for four months.
   22 stenographers were hired, each at the rate of $30,000 a year, for three months.
The total amount paid to these temporary employees was MOST NEARLY

   A. $1,780,000
   B. $450,000
   C. $650,000
   D. $390,000

24. Assume that there are 2,300 employees in a city agency. Also, assume that five percent of these employees are accountants, that 80 percent of the accountants have college degrees, and that one-half of the accountants who have college degrees have five years of experience. Then, the number of employees in the agency who are accountants with college degrees and five years of experience is

   A. 46   B. 51   C. 460   D. 920

25. Assume that the regular 8-hour working day of a laborer is from 8 A.M. to 5 P.M., with an hour off for lunch. He earns a regular hourly rate of pay for these 8 hours and is paid at the rate of time-and-a-half for each hour worked after his regular working day.
If, on a certain day, he works from 8 A.M. to 6 P.M., with an hour off for lunch, and earns $171, his regular hourly rate of pay is

   A. $16.30   B. $17.10   C. $18.00   D. $19.00

KEY (CORRECT ANSWERS)

1. A
2. D
3. C
4. A
5. C
6. D
7. D
8. B
9. A
10. C

11. A
12. B
13. D
14. C
15. D
16. B
17. B
18. A
19. C
20. B

21. A
22. C
23. B
24. A
25. C

SOLUTIONS TO PROBLEMS

1. 28/112 is equivalent to 1:4

2. Maximum number of folders = (10)(25)(5) = 1250

3. Average annual increase = ($25,107-19,353) ÷ 7 = $822

4. $1,457,400 - (55)($16,800) = $533,400 = total amount paid to senior clerks. Average senior clerk's salary = $533,400 ÷ 28 = $19,050

5. Number of words on 3rd page = 954 - 283 - 366 = 305

6. Clerk A processed (40)(1.30) = 52 forms and clerk C processed (52)(1.25) = 65 forms. Finally, 65 - 40 = 25

7. Take-home pay = $678 - (.15)($678) - (.025)($678) - $1.95 - $9.00 = $548.40

8. (400)(12) = 4800 pencils. In 2002, (3/4)(4800) = 3600 were used, so that 1200 pencils were available at the beginning of 2003. Since 3600 pencils were also used in 2003, the agency had to buy 3600 - 1200 = 2400 pencils.

9. Average salary for clerk in Agency X = ($15,105+$15,750+$16,440)/3 = $15,765. Average salary for clerk in Agency Y = ($15,825+ $15,825+$16,086) ÷ 3 = $15,912. Difference in average salaries = $147.

10. Total pay = ($13.60)(40) + ($20.40)(5) = $646.00

11. In 2005, amount spent = $156,500 ÷ 1.12 ≈ $139,730 (Actual value = $139,732.1429)

12. At the end of 2 hours, (1100)(2) + (1450)(2) + (1200)(2) + (1300X2) + (1250X2) = 12,600 letters have been inserted into envelopes. The remaining 11,400 letters done by clerks A, B, and C will require 11,400 ÷ (1100+1450+1250) = 3 hours.

13. 60 ÷ .40 = 150

14. 96 ÷ 3/8 = (96)(8/3) = 256

15. Total cost = (5)[(25)(.20)+(35)(.30)+(350)(.40)]= $777.50

16. In 1998, (12,000) (1.25) = 15,000 applications were issued In 1996, (15,000)(.90) = 13,500 applications were issued

17. Total number of hours = $\frac{120}{40} + \frac{80}{20} = 7$

18. (.75)(500 dozen) = 375 dozen purchased in 2000 at a cost of ($1.20)(1.20) = $1.44 per dozen. Total cost for 2000 = ($1.44) (375) = $540

19. Total time = 1 hour + 450/75 hrs. = 7 hours

20. (.30)(420) - (1/7)(420) = 126 - 60 = 66

21. Cost per minute = (120)(.02) = $2.40. Then, $12 ÷ $2.40 = 5 minutes

22. (32)(22) ÷ 16 = 44 clerks

23. Total amount paid = (20)($27,500)(2/12) + (18)($31,500)(4/12) + (22)($30,000)(3/12) = $445,666.$\overline{6}$ ≈ $450,000

24. Number of accountants with college degrees and five years of experience = (2300)(.05)(.80)(1/2) = 46

25. Let x = regular hourly pay. Then, (8)(x) + (1)(1.5x) = $1.71 So, 9.5x = 171. Solving, x = $18

TEST 2

DIRECTIONS: Each question or incomplete statement is followed by several suggested answers or completions. Select the one that BEST answers the question or completes the statement. *PRINT THE LETTER OF THE CORRECT ANSWER IN THE SPACE AT THE RIGHT.*

1. Assume that you know the capacity of a filing cabinet, the extent of which it is filled, and the daily rate at which material is being added to the file.
   In order to estimate how many more days it will take for the cabinet to be filled to capacity, you should

   A. divide the extent to which the cabinet is filled by the daily rate
   B. take the difference between the capacity of the cabinet and the material in it, and multiply the result by the daily rate of adding material
   C. divide the daily rate of adding material by the difference between the capacity of the cabinet and the material in it
   D. take the difference between the capacity of the cabinet and the material in it, and divide the result by the daily rate of adding material

   1.____

2. Suppose you have been asked to compute the average salary earned in your department during the past year. For each of the divisions of the department, you are given the number of employees and the average salary.
   In order to find the requested overall average salary for the department, you should

   A. add the average salaries of the various divisions and divide the total by the number of divisions
   B. multiply the number of employees in each division by the corresponding average salary, add the results and divide the total by the number of employees in the department
   C. add the average salaries of the various divisions and divide the total by the total number of employees in the department
   D. multiply the sum of the average salaries of the various divisions by the total number of divisions and divide the resulting product by the total number of employees in the department

   2.____

3. Suppose that a group of six clerks has been assigned to assemble the duplicated pages of a report into completed copies. After four hours of work, they have been able to complete one-third of the job.
   In order to assemble all the remaining copies in three more hours of work, the number of clerks which will have to be added to the original six, assuming that all the clerks assigned to this task work at the same rate of speed, is

   A. 10   B. 16   C. 2   D. 6

   3.____

4. A study of the grades of students in a certain college revealed that in 2005, 15% fewer students received a passing grade in mathematics than in 2004, whereas in 2006 the number of students passing mathematics increased 15% over 2005.
   On the basis of this study, it would be MOST accurate to conclude that

   A. the same percentage of students passed mathematics in 2004 as in 2006
   B. of the three years studied, the greatest percentage of students passed mathematics in 2006

   4.____

179

C. the percentage of students who passed mathematics in 2006 was less than the percentage passing this subject in 2004
D. the percentage of students passing mathematics in 2004 was 15% greater than the percentage of students passing this subject in 2006

5. A city department employs 1,400 people, of whom 35% are clerks and 1/8 are stenographers.
   The number of employees in the department who are neither clerks nor stenographers is

   A. 640   B. 665   C. 735   D. 760

6. Assume that there are 190 papers to be filed and that Clerk A and Clerk B are assigned to file these papers. If Clerk A files 40 papers more than Clerk B, then the number of papers that Clerk A files is

   A. 75   B. 110   C. 115   D. 150

7. A stock clerk had on hand the following items:
   500 pads, each worth 16 cents
   130 pencils, each worth 12 cents
   50 dozen rubber bands, worth 8 cents a dozen
   If, from this stock, he issued 125 pads, 45 pencils, and 48 rubber bands, the value of the remaining stock would be

   A. $25.72   B. $27.80   C. $70.52   D. $73.88

8. In a particular agency, there were 160 accidents in 2002. Of these accidents, 75% were due to unsafe acts and the rest were due to unsafe conditions. In the following year, a special safety program was established. The number of accidents in 2004 due to unsafe acts was reduced to 35% of what it had been in 2002.
   How many accidents due to unsafe acts were there in 2004?

   A. 20   B. 36   C. 42   D. 56

9. At the end of every month, the petty cash fund of Agency A is reimbursed for payments made from the fund during the month. During the month of February, the amounts paid from the fund were entered on receipts as follows: 10 bus fares of $1.40 each and one taxi fare of $14.00. At the end of the month, the money left in the fund was in the following denominations: 60 one-dollar bills, 16 quarters, 40 dimes, and 80 nickels.
   If the petty cash fund is reduced by 20% for the following month, how much money will there be available in the petty cash fund for March?

   A. $44   B. $80   C. $86   D. $100

10. An employee worked on a job for 6 weeks, 5 days per week, and 8 hours per day. How many hours did he work on the job?

    A. 40   B. 48   C. 55   D. 240

11. Divide 35 by .7.

    A. 5   B. 42   C. 50   D. 245

12. .1% of 25 =

    A. .025 B. .25 C. 2.5 D. 25

13. In a city agency, 80 percent of the total number of employees are more than 25 years of age and 65 percent of the total number of employees are high school graduates.
    The SMALLEST possible percent of employees who are both high school graduates and more than 25 years of age is

    A. 35% B. 45% C. 55% D. 65%

14. Two clerical units, X and Y, each having a different number of clerks, are assigned to file registration cards. It takes Unit X, which contains 8 clerks, 21 days to file the same number of cards that Unit Y can file in 28 days. It is also a fact that Unit X can file 174,528 cards in 72 days.
    Assuming that all the clerks in both units work at the same rate of speed, the number of cards which can be filed by Unit Y in 144 days, if 4 more clerks are added to the staff of Unit Y, is MOST NEARLY

    A. 392,000 B. 436,000 C. 523,000 D. 669,000

15. Assume that two machines, each costing $14,750, were purchased for your office. Each machine requires the services of an operator at a salary of $2,000 per month. These machines are to replace six clerks, two of whom earn $1,550 per month each, and four of whom earn $1,700 per month each.
    The number of months it will take for the cost of the machines to be made up from the savings in salaries is

    A. less than four B. four
    C. five   D. more than five

16. Suppose that the amount of stationery used by your department in August decreased by 16% as compared with the amount used in July, and that the amount used in September increased by 25% as compared with the amount used in August.
    The amount of stationery used in September as compared with the amount used in July is

    A. greater by 5 percent B. less by 5 percent
    C. greater by 9 percent D. the same

17. An employee earns $48 a day and works 5 days a week.
    He will earn $2,160 in _____ weeks.

    A. 5 B. 7 C. 8 D. 9

18. In a certain bureau, the entire staff consists of 1 senior supervisor, 2 supervisors, 6 assistant supervisors, and 54 associate workers.
    The percent of the staff who are not associate workers is MOST NEARLY

    A. 14 B. 21 C. 27 D. 32

19. In a certain bureau, five employees each earn $1,000 a month, another 3 employees each earn $2,200 a month, and another two employees each earn $1,400 a month.
    The monthly payroll for these employees is

    A. $3,600 B. $8,800 C. $11,400 D. $14,400

20. An employee contributes 5% of his salary to the pension fund.
    If his salary is $1,200 a month, the amount of his contribution to the pension fund in a year is

    A. $480   B. $720   C. $960   D. $1,200

21. The number of square feet in an area that is 50 feet long and 30 feet wide is

    A. 80   B. 150   C. 800   D. 1,500

22. A farm hand was paid a weekly wage of $332.16 for a 48-hour work week. As a result of a new labor contract, he is paid $344.96 a week for a 44-hour work week with time and one-half pay for time worked in excess of 44 hours in any work week.
    If he continues to work 48 hours weekly under the new contract, the amount by which his average hourly rate for a 48-hour work week under the new contract exceeds the hourly rate previously paid him lies between _____ and _____ cents, inclusive.

    A. 91;100   B. 101;110   C. 111;120   D. 121;130

23. Each side of a square room, which is being used as an office, measures 66 feet. The floor of the room is divided by six traffic aisles, each aisle being six feet wide. Three of the aisles run parallel to the east and west sides of the room, and the other three run parallel to the north and south sides of the room, so that the remaining floor space is divided into 16 equal sections. If all of the floor space which is not being used for traffic aisles is occupied by desk and chair sets, and each set takes up 24 square feet of floor space, the number of desk and chair sets in the room is

    A. 80   B. 64   C. 36   D. 96

24. In 2005, a city agency bought 12,000 envelopes at $4.00 per hundred. In 2006, the price of envelopes purchased was 40 percent higher than the 2005 price, but only 60 percent as many envelopes were bought.
    The total cost of the envelopes purchased in 2006 was MOST NEARLY

    A. $250   B. $320   C. $400   D. $480

25. In a city agency, 25 percent of the women employees and 50 percent of the men employees attended a general staff meeting.
    If 48 percent of all the employees in the agency are women, the percentage of all the employees who attended the meeting is

    A. 36%   B. 37%   C. 38%   D. 75%

KEY (CORRECT ANSWERS)

1.	D	11.	C
2.	B	12.	A
3.	A	13.	B
4.	C	14.	A
5.	C	15.	C
6.	C	16.	A
7.	D	17.	D
8.	C	18.	A
9.	B	19.	D
10.	D	20.	B

21. D
22. D
23. D
24. C
25. C

SOLUTIONS TO PROBLEMS

1. To determine number of days required to fill cabinet to capacity, subtract material in it from capacity amount, then divide by daily rate of adding material. Example: A cabinet already has 10 folders in it, and the capacity is 100 folders. Suppose 5 folders per day are added. Number of days to fill to capacity = (100-10) ÷ 5 = 18

2. To determine overall average salary, multiply number of employees in each division by that division's average salary, add results, then divide by total number of employees. Example: Division A has 4 employees with average salary of $40,000; division B has 6 employees with average salary of $36,000; division C has 2 employees with average salary of $46,000. Average salary = [(4)($40,000)+(6)($36,000)+(2)($46,000)] / 12 = $39,000

3. (6)(4) = 24 clerk-hours. Since only one-third of work has been done, (24) (3) - 24 = 48 clerk-hours remain. Then, 48 3 = 16 clerks. Thus, 16 - 6 = 10 additional clerks.

4. The percentage of students passing math in 2006 was less than the percentage of those passing math in 2004. Example: Suppose 400 students passed math in 2004. Then, (400)(.85) = 340 passed in 2005. Finally, (340)(1.15) = 391 passed in 2006.

5. 1400 - (.35)(1400) - (1/8)(1400) = 735

6. Let x = number of papers filed by clerk A, x-40 = number of papers filed by clerk B. Then, x + (x-40) = 190 Solving, x = 115

7. (500-125)(.16) + (130-45)(.12) + (50 - 48/12)(.08) = $60.00 + $10.20 + $3.68 = $73.88

8. (160)(.75) = 120 accidents due to unsafe acts in 2002. In 2004, (120)(.35) = 42 accidents due to unsafe acts

9. Original amount at beginning of February in the fund = (10)($1.40) + (1)($14.00) + (60)($1) + (16)(.25) + (40)(.10) + (80)(.05) = $100. Finally, for March, ($100)(.80) = $80 will be available

10. Total hours = (6)(5)(8) = 240

11. 35 ÷ .7 = 50

12. .1% of 25 = (.001)(25) = .025

13. Let A = percent of employees who are at least 25 years old and B = percent of employees who are high school graduates. Also, let N = percent of employees who fit neither category and J = percent of employees who are in both categories.
Then, 100 = A + B + N - J. Substituting, 100 = 80 + 65 + N - J To minimize J, let N = 0. So, 100 = 80 + 65 + 0 - J. Solving, J = 45

14. Let Y = number of clerks in Unit Y. Then, (8)(21) = (4)(28), so Y = 6. Unit X has 8 clerks who can file 174,528 cards in 72 flays; thus, each clerk in Unit X can file 174,528 ÷ 72 ÷ 8 = 303 cards per day. Adding 4 clerks to Unit Y will yield 10 clerks in that unit. Since their rate is equal to that of Unit X, the clerks in Unit Y will file, in 144 days, is (303)(10)(144) = 436,320 ≈ 436,000 cards.

15. Let x = required number of months. The cost of the machines in x months = (2)(14,750) + (2)(2000)(x) = 29,500 + 4000x. The savings in salaries for the displaced clerks = x[(2)(1550) +(4)(1700)] = 9900x. Thus, 29,500 + 4000x = 9900x. Solving, x = 5. So, five months will elapse in order to achieve a savings in cost.

16. Let x = amount used in July, so that .84x = amount used in August. For September, the amount used = (.84x)(1.25) = 1.05x. This means the amount used in September is 5% more than the amount used in July.

17. Each week he earns ($48)(5) = $240. Then, $2160 ÷ $240 = 9 weeks

18. (1+2+6) ÷ 63 = 1/7 ≈ 14%

19. Monthly payroll = (5)($1000) + (3)($2200) + (2)($1400) = $14,400

20. Yearly contribution to pension fund = (12)($1200)(.05) = $720

21. (50')(30') = 1500 sq.ft.

22. Old rate = 332.16 ÷ 48 = 6.92 (48 hours)
    New rate = 344.96 (44 hours)
    Overtime rate = 344.96 ÷ 44 = 7.75/hr. x 1.5 x 4 = 46.48
    344.96 + 46.48 = 391.44
    391.44 ÷ 48 = 8.15
    815 - 692 = 123 cents an hour more

23. Each of the 16 sections is a square with side [66'-(3)(6')] ÷ 4 = 12'. So each section contains (12')(12') = 144 sq.ft.
    The number of desk and chair sets = (144 ÷ 24) (16) = 96

24. In 2006, (.60)(12,000) = 7200 envelopes were bought and the price per hundred was ($4.00)(1.40) = $5.60. The total cost = (5.60)(72) = $403.20 ≈ $400

25. (.25)(.48) + (.50)(.52) = .38 = 38%

TEST 3

DIRECTIONS: Each question or incomplete statement is followed by several suggested answers or completions. Select the one that BEST answers the question or completes the statement. *PRINT THE LETTER OF THE CORRECT ANSWER IN THE SPACE AT THE RIGHT.*

1. According to one suggested filing system, no more than 12 folders should be filed behind any one file guide and from 10 to 20 file guides should be used in each file drawer. Based on this filing system, the MAXIMUM number of folders that a four-drawer file cabinet can hold is

    A. 240   B. 480   C. 960   D. 1,200

2. A certain office uses three different forms. Last year, it used 3,500 copies of Form L, 6,700 copies of Form M, and 10,500 copies of Form P. This year, the office expects to decrease the use of each of these forms by 5%. The TOTAL number of these three forms which the office expects to use this year is

    A. 10,350   B. 16,560   C. 19,665   D. 21,735

3. The hourly rate of pay for a certain part-time employee is computed by dividing his yearly salary rate by the number of hours in the work year. The employee's yearly salary rate is $18,928, and there are 1,820 hours in the work year.
   If this employee works 18 hours during one week, his TOTAL earnings for these 18 hours are

    A. $180.00   B. $183.60   C. $187.20   D. $190.80

4. Assume that the regular work week of an employee is 35 hours and that the employee is paid for any extra hours worked according to the following schedule. For hours worked in excess of 35 hours, up to and including 40 hours, the employee receives his regular hourly rate of pay. For hours worked in excess of 40 hours, the employee receives 1 1/2 times his hourly rate of pay.
   If the employee's hourly rate of pay is $11.20 and he works 43 hours during a certain week, his TOTAL pay for the week would be

    A. $481.60   B. $498.40   C. $556.00   D. $722.40

5. A clerk divided his 35 hour work week as follows:
   1/5 of his time in sorting mail;
   1/2 of his time in filing letters; and
   1/7 of his time in reception work.
   The rest of his time was devoted to messenger work. The percentage of time spent on messenger work by the clerk during the week was MOST NEARLY

    A. 6%   B. 10%   C. 14%   D. 16%

6. A city department has set up a computing unit and has rented 5 computing machines at a yearly rental of $700 per machine. In addition, the cost to the department for the maintenance and repair of each of these machines is $50 per year. Five computing machine operators, each receiving an annual salary of $15,000, and a supervisor, who receives $19,000 a year, have been assigned to this unit. This unit will perform the work previously performed by 10 employees whose combined salary was $162,000 a year.
   On the basis of these facts, the savings that will result from the operation of this computing unit for 5 years will be MOST NEARLY

    A. $250,000   B. $320,000   C. $330,000   D. $475,000

7. Twelve clerks are assigned to enter certain data on index cards. This number of clerks could perform the task in 18 days. After these clerks have worked on this assignment for 6 days, 4 more clerks are added to the staff to do this work.
   Assuming that all the clerks work at the same rate of speed, the entire task, instead of taking 18 days, will be performed in _____ days.

   A. 9   B. 12   C. 15   D. 16

8. Suppose that a file cabinet, which has a capacity of 3,000 cards, now contains approximately 2,200 cards. Cards are added to the file at the average rate of 30 cards a day.
   To find the number of days it will take to fill the cabinet to capacity,

   A. divide 3,000 by 30
   B. divide 2,200 by 3,000
   C. divide 800 by 30
   D. multiply 30 by the fraction 2,200 divided by 3,000

9. Six gross of special drawing pencils were purchased for use in a city department.
   If the pencils were used at the rate of 24 a week, the MAXIMUM number of weeks that the six gross of pencils would last is _____ weeks.

   A. 6   B. 12   C. 24   D. 36

10. A stock clerk had 600 pads on hand. He then issued 3/8 of his supply of pads to Division X, 1/4 to Division Y, and 1/6 to Division Z.
    The number of pads remaining in stock is

    A. 48   B. 125   C. 240   D. 475

11. If a certain job can be performed by 18 clerks in 26 days, the number of clerks needed to perform the job in 12 days is _____ clerks.

    A. 24   B. 30   C. 39   D. 52

12. In anticipation of a seasonal increase in the amount of work to be performed by his division, a division chief prepared the following list of additional temporary employees needed by his division and the amount of time they would be employed:
    26 cashiers, each at $24,000 a year, for 2 months
    15 laborers, each at $85.00 a day, for 50 days
    6 clerks, each at $21,000 a year, for 3 months
    The total approximate cost for this additional personnel would be MOST NEARLY

    A. $200,000   B. $250,000   C. $500,000   D. $600,000

13. A copy machine company offered to sell a city agency 4 copy machines at a discount of 15% from the list price, and to allow the agency $850 for each of its two old machines. The list price of the new machines is $6,250 per machine.
    If the city agency accepts this offer, the amount of money it will have to provide for the purchase of these 4 machines is

    A. $17,350   B. $22,950   C. $19,550   D. $18,360

14. A stationery buyer was offered bond paper at the following price scale:
    $1.43 per ream for the first 1,000 reams
    $1.30 per ream for the next 4,000 reams
    $1.20 per ream for each additional ream beyond 5,000 reams
    If the buyer ordered 10,000 reams of paper, the average cost per ream, computed to the nearest cent, was

    A. $1.24   B. $1.26   C. $1.31   D. $1.36

15. A clerk has 5.70 percent of his salary deducted for his retirement pension. If this clerk's annual salary is $20,400, the monthly deduction for his retirement pension is

    A. $298.20   B. $357.90   C. $1,162.80   D. $96.90

16. In a certain bureau, two-thirds of the employees are clerks and the remainder are typists. If there are 90 clerks, then the number of typists in this bureau is

    A. 135   B. 45   C. 120   D. 30

17. The number of investigations conducted by an agency in 1999 was 3,600. In 2000, the number of investigations conducted was one-third more than in 1999. The number of investigations conducted in 2001 was three-fourths of the number conducted in 2000. It is anticipated that the number of investigations conducted in 2002 will be equal to the average of the three preceding years. On the basis of this information, the MOST accurate of the following statements is that the number of investigations conducted in

    A. 1999 is larger than the number anticipated for 2002
    B. 2000 is smaller than the number anticipated for 2002
    C. 2001 is equal to the number conducted in 1999
    D. 2001 is larger than the number anticipated in 2002

18. A city agency engaged in repair work uses a small part which the city purchases for 14 each. Assume that, in a certain year, the total expenditure of the city for this part was $700.
    How many of these parts were purchased that year?

    A. 50   B. 200   C. 2,000   D. 5,000

19. The work unit which you supervise is responsible for processing 15 reports per month. If your unit has 4 clerks and the best worker completes 40% of the reports himself, how many reports would each of the other clerks have to complete if they all do an equal number?

    A. 1   B. 2   C. 3   D. 4

20. Assume that the work unit in which you work has 24 clerks and 18 stenographers. In order to change the ratio of stenographers to clerks so that there is 1 stenographer for every 4 clerks, it would be necessary to REDUCE the number of stenographers by

    A. 3   B. 6   C. 9   D. 12

21. The arithmetic mean salary for five employees earning $18,500, $18,300, $18,600, $18,400, and $18,500, respectively, is

    A. $18,450   B. $18,460   C. $18,475   D. $18,500

22. Last year, a city department which is responsible for purchasing supplies ordered bond paper in equal quantities from 22 different companies. The price was exactly the same for each company, and the total cost for the 22 orders was $693,113.
    Assuming prices did not change during the year, the cost of each order was MOST NEARLY

    A. $31,490   B. $31,495   C. $31,500   D. $31,505

23. Suppose that a large bureau has 187 employees. On a particular day, approximately 14% of these employees are not available for work because of absences due to vacation, illness, or other reasons. Of the remaining employees, 1/7 are assigned to a special project while the balance are assigned to the normal work of the bureau. The number of employees assigned to the normal work of the bureau on that day is

    A. 112   B. 124   C. 138   D. 142

24. Suppose that you are in charge of a typing pool of 8 typists. Two typists type at the rate of 38 words per minute; three type at the rate of 40 words per minute; three type at the rate of 42 words per minute. The average typewritten page consists of 50 lines, 12 words per line. Each employee works from 9 to 5 with one hour off for lunch.
    The total number of pages typed by this pool in one day is, on the average, CLOSEST to _____ pages.

    A. 205   B. 225   C. 250   D. 275

25. Suppose that part-time workers are paid $7.20 an hour, prorated to the nearest half hour, with pay guaranteed for a minimum of four hours if services are required for less than four hours. In one operation, part-time workers signed the time sheet as follows:

Worker	In	Out
A	8:00 A.M.	11:35 A.M.
B	8:30 A.M.	3:20 P.M.
C	7:55 A.M.	11:00 A.M.
D	8:30 A.M.	2:25 P.M.

    How much would TOTAL payment to these part-time workers amount to for this operation, assuming that those who stayed after 12 Noon were not paid for one hour which they took off for lunch?

    A. $134.40   B. $136.80   C. $142.20   D. $148.80

KEY (CORRECT ANSWERS)

1.	C	11.	C
2.	C	12.	A
3.	C	13.	C
4.	B	14.	B
5.	D	15.	D
6.	B	16.	B
7.	C	17.	C
8.	C	18.	D
9.	D	19.	C
10.	B	20.	D

21. B
22. D
23. C
24. B
25. B

SOLUTIONS TO PROBLEMS

1. Maximum number of folders = (4)(12)(20) = 960

2. (3500+6700+10,500)(.95) = 19,665

3. Hourly rate = $18,928 ÷ 1820 = $10.40. Then, the pay for 18 hours = ($10.40)(18) = $187.20

4. Total pay = ($11.20)(40) + ($11.20)(1.5)(3) = $498.40

5. (1 - 1/5 - 1/2 - 1/7)(100)% ≈ 16%

6. Previous cost for five years = ($324,000)(5) = $1,620,000
   Present cost for five years = (5)(5)($1,400) + (5)(5)($100) + (5)(5)($30,000) + (1)(5)($38,000) = $977,500   The net savings = $642,500 ≈ $640,000

7. (12)(18) = 216 clerk-days. Then, 216 - (12)(6) = 144 clerk-days of work left when 4 more clerks are added. Now, 16 clerks will finish the task in 144 ÷ 16 = 9 more days. Finally, the task will require a total of 6 + 9 = 15 days.

8. Number of days needed = (3000-2200) ÷ 30 = 26.7, which is equivalent to dividing 800 by 30.

9. (6)(144) = 864 pencils purchased. Then, 864 ÷ 24 = 36 maximum number of weeks

10. Number of remaining pads = 600 - (1)(600) - (1/4)(600) - (1/6)(600) = 125

11. (18)(26) ÷ 12 = 39 clerks

12. Total cost = (26)($24,000)(2/12) + (15)($85)(50) + (6)($21,000)(3/12) = $199,250 $200,000

13. (4)($6250)(.85) - (2)($850) = $19,550

14. Total cost = ($1.43)(1000) + ($1.30)(4000) + ($1.20X5000) = $12,630. Average cost per ream = $12,630 10,000 ≈ $1.26

15. Monthly salary = $20,400 ÷ 12 = $1700. Thus, the monthly deduction for his pension = ($1700)(.057) + $96.90

16. Number of employees = 90 ÷ 2/3 = 135. Then, the number of typists = (1/3)(135) = 45

17. The number of investigations for each year is as follows:
    1999: 3600
    2000: (3600)(1 1/3) = 4800
    2001: (4800)(3/4) = 3600
    2002: (3600+4800+3600)/3 = 4000
    So, the number of investigations were equal for 1999 and 2001.

18. $700 ÷ .14 = 5000 parts

19. The best worker does (.40)(15) = 6 reports. The other 9 reports are divided equally among the other 3 clerks, so each clerk does 9 ÷ 3 = 3 reports.

20. 1:4 = 6:24 . Thus, the number of stenographers must be reduced by 18 - 6 = 12

21. Mean = ($18,500+$18,300+$18,400+$18,500) ÷ 5 = $18,460

22. The cost per order = $693,113 ÷ 22 ≈ $31,505

23. 187 - (.14) = 26. 187 - 26 = 161 - 1/7 (161) = 23
    161 - 23 = 138

24. Number of words typed in 1 min. = (2)(38) + (3)(40) + (3)(42) = 322. For 7 hours, the total number of words typed = (7)(60)(322) = 135,240. Each page contains (on the average) (50)(12) = 600 words. Finally, 135,240 ÷ 600 ≈ 225 pages

25. Worker A = ($7.20)(4) = $28.80
    Worker B = ($7.20)(3 1/2) + ($7.20)(2 1/2) = $43.20
    Worker C = ($7.20)(4) = $28.80
    Worker D = ($7.20)(3 1/2) + ($7.20)(1 1/2) = $36.00
    Total for all 4 workers = $136.80
    Note: Workers A and C received the guaranteed minimum 4 hours pay each.

PRINCIPLES AND PRACTICES OF TRANSCRIPTION

TABLE OF CONTENTS

		Page
I.	30 RULES FOR CORRECT TRANSCRIPTION	1
II.	LIST OF DIVISION DEMONS IN TRANSCRIPTION (WITH ACCENT MARKS)	3
	Abate................Axiomatic	3
	Bacteria............Demonstrative	4
	Deodorant........Itinerary	5
	Jovial...............yeoma	6
	Strenuous.........Zoology	7

PRINCIPLES AND PRACTICES OF TRANSCRIPTION

I. 30 RULES FOR CORRECT TRANSCRIPTION

1. *CORRECT:* Type date on one line
    INCORRECT: Break the date up, as: May 15,1968

2. *CORRECT:* Type Mr. James Doe on one line.
    INCORRECT: Break it up, as: Mr. James Doe

3. *CORRECT:* Type address together.
    INCORRECT: Break the address up, as: 42 Sixth Avenue.

4. *CORRECT:* Divide a word so that more than one letter is on a line.
    INCORRECT: Divide the word so that only one letter is on a line, as: a-lone.

5. *CORRECT:* Divide a word so that more than two letters are on the following line.
    INCORRECT: Divide a word so that two letters remain on the second line, as remind-ed.

6. Both enclosed and inclosed are correct. Make sure that Enc. or Inc. under the initials match the word in the letter.

7. *CORRECT:* Copy the address from a letter or information sheet correctly. For instance, if Mr. Elliott Davis is in the letter or sheet (two 1's), copy it exactly.
    INCORRECT: Type Eliott with one l.

8. Type My dear Sir:-- dear with a small d.

9. Use a number for the date when the month is typed first, as May 3. Otherwise, write the number in word form: for example, the third of May.

10. Leave off st, nd, rd, th, from the number if the month is typed first; for example, May 1, May 2, May 3, May 4.

11. A medium-sized letter should have at least two paragraphs. Sometimes a short note or letter will have only one paragraph. Indicate a new paragraph when the thought changes.

12. Type the dictator's initials and your initials four single spaces below the complimentary closing. Enc. or Inc. is typed directly below the initials.

13. *CORRECT:* ype Fifth Avenue, rather than 5th Avenue.
    INCORRECT: Write 5th in your shorthand notes as the letters that would be considered longhand. The $ sign and % sign are considered longhand, too.

14. *CORRECT:* Use the MR key when erasing.
    INCORRECT: Erase over the key basket.

15. Clean up your letter before handing it in. Erase smudge marks and other marks which detract from the attractiveness of your work.

16. Check each letter before removing it from the machine. Check word for word with your stenography notes.

17. *CORRECT:* Use your dictionary if you are not sure of a spelling or word division.
    INCORRECT: Guess at spelling or word division.

18. Don't overpunctuate. "When in doubt, leave it out" is a good rule to follow. Too many commas are wrong - and in poor taste.

19. When expressions such as: of course, no doubt, therefore, however, etc., occur in the middle of a sentence, use commas before and after. One comma is incorrect. If a sentence should begin with these words, always put a comma immediately after the expression, as: Therefore, we ask that you call us as soon as you can.

20. Whenever a sentence ends, space twice before starting the next sentence. However, after a semi-colon, comma, or abbreviation (Mr.) leave one space.

21. Words or phrases in a series are separated by commas, as: The colors of our flag are red, white, and blue.

22. After an introductory clause, use a comma, as: Since you were here, many things have changed.

23. When two independent clauses are joined by <u>and</u>, <u>but</u>, <u>or</u>,--use a comma after the first clause, as: I expect to see you, and I hope you will be on time.

24. Words starting with <u>over</u> or <u>under</u> are spelled as one word, as overpaid, overdue, oversight, overwork, underpaid, undersell, undertones.

25. When two or more words are used as a single adjective to describe a noun following immediately, hyphenate, as: up-to-date home, first-class mail, low-priced articles. However, if the noun does not follow immediately, omit the hyphen, as: a home that is up to date.

26. If several adjectives are used to describe one noun, treat as you would words in a series, as: a warm, red coat.

27. Don't divide a word that already has a hyphen, as: self-control.

28. <u>Passed</u> is a verb. When we refer to a bill that is <u>past</u> due, we are referring to a matter of time.

29. Eliminate "flying" capitals by holding your shift key down a trifle longer.

30. When you are comparing something, use <u>than</u>. <u>Then</u> refers to time. 'For example: more than, better than, prettier than, smaller than.
   Get your mother's permission, and <u>then</u> we can go on a trip. She pays less rent <u>than</u> you.

II. LIST OF DIVISION DEMONS IN TRANSCRIPTION (WITH ACCENT MARKS)

a bate'	ag' ri cul ture	a' pri cot
ata do' men	a larm'	ar' bi trar y
a bom' i na ble	a' li as	ar cade'
ab' ro gate	al' ien ate	ar' chi tec ture
ab sen tee'	al' i mon y	ar' du ous
ab' so lute ly	al lies'	a' ri a
ab sorb'	al read' y	a ris' to crat
ab' sti nence	am a teur'	ar ma' da
ab surd'	am bi gu' i ty	ar' ro gance
ac a dem' ic	a men' i ty	a skance'
ac eel' er ate	A mer' i can	a skew'
ac ces' so ry	a' mi a ble	as pir' ant
ac cli' mate	am ne' si a	as' ter isk
ac com' pa nist	an' arch y	ath' lete
a cu' men	an ces' tral	ath let' ics
ad' a mant	an' ec dote	a torn' ic
ad dress'	an ni' hi late	au da' cious
a dept'	an nu' i ty	au di to' ri urn
ad' mi ra ble	an tag' o nist	au gust'
ad o les' cent	an te ced' ent	aunt
ad vance'	an tic' i pate	a vi a' tion
ad' ver sar y	ap a thet' ic	a' vi a tor
ad ver' tise ment	ap pa ra' tus	ax i o mat' i c
af fi da' vit	ap par' ent	
a' gen cy	ap' pli ca ble	
ag gres' sor	ap pro ba' tion	

4

bac te′ ri a
bade
bal′ let
bal′ lot
ban′ quet
bap′ tism
bar′ ba rous
be cause′
bel lig′ er ent
ben e fi′ ci ar y
be nev′ o lent
be troth′ al
be yond′
bi′ as
bi en′ ni al
big′ a my
big′ ot ry
bi og′ ra phy
bi tu′ mi nous
bi zarre′
black′ guard
bias′ phe my
bludg′ oen
bo le′ ro
bou′ doir
bour geois′
bra va′ do
brig′ and
bron′ chi al
bru nette′
buc ca neer′
bu reauc′ ra cy

cab′ a ret
caf e te′ ri a
can′ o py

ca price′
car′ a mel
car′ a van
car′ i ca ture
car′ ni val
cas′ se role
ca tas′ tro phe
cat′ e go ry
cav i ar′
ce leb′ ri ty
ce ment′
cen trif′ u gal
cha grin′
cha let′
cham′ ois
cham′ pi on
cha ot′ ic
chasm
chas′ tise ment
chauf feur′
chi can′ er y
chiv′ al ric
chrys an′ the mum
cig a rette′
clan des′ tine
clean′ li ness
clem′ en cy
cli che′
cli en tele′
clique
co a li′ tion
coif fure′
col lo′ qui al
colo′ nel
co los′ sal
com′ bat ant

com′ fort a ble
com mu ni que′
com′ pa ra ble
com′ pe tent
com pla′ cent
con cer′ to
con coct′
con do′ lence
con gen′ ial
con nois seur′
con ta′ gious
con tern′ po rar y
con tin′ u ous
con′ tro ver sy
con′ ver sant
co quette′
cor′ o net
cor′ pu lent
cos turn′ er
cou′ pon
cov′ et ous
cred′ u lous
cri te′ ri on
cu′ bi cle
cu′ li nar y
deaf
de bate′
de but′
dec′ ade
de dine′
dec′ o rous
de co′ rum
def′ i cit
del i ca tes′ sen
de lin′ quent
de mon′ stra tive

de o' dor ant
de plor' a ble
de pos' i tor
de' pot
dep ri va' tion
der' e lict
des' pi ca ble
det' ri ment
di' a mond
di' a per
die ta' tor
di gress'
di late'
di lem' ma
di' o cese
di plo' ma
di plo' ma cy
dir' i gi ble
dis as' ter
dis cern'
dis cre' tion
di shev' el
dis in' ter est ed
dis par' age
dis' pu ta ble
dis' si pate
dis tin' guish
di vulge'
doc' ile
dog' ged
dog' ma
dom' i cile
du' bi ous

ec cen' trie
e con' o my
ec' sta sy
e' diet
ef feet'
e' go tist
e lee' toral
em' a nate
em ploy ee'
en cy clo pe' di a
en' er gy
en' ter prise
en tire'
en vel' opv-(y.)
en' ve lope (n .)
en vi' ron ment

ep' i cure
e qua to' ri al
eg' ui ta ble
eq' ui ty
er ro' ne ous
es' pi o nage
eth' ics
et' i quette
eu' lo gy
eu' phe mism
ev' i dent ly
ex as' per ated
ex cise'
ex' i gen cies
ex' o dus
ex og' a my
ex ot' ic
ex pe' di ent
ex pense'
ex per' i ment
ex' qui site
ex tra' ne ous
ex' tri cate
fac sim' i le
fau' cet
Feb' ru ar y
fi as' co
fie ti' tious
fig' ur a tive
fil' i bus ter film
fi na' le
fin an cier'
fi nesse'
for bade'
fore' head
fore' most
for' mi da ble
frag' ile
frag' men tar y
frus tra' tion
fu' tile
ga' la
gal' ax y
ga rage'
gen' u ine
gi gan' tic
gov' ern ment

griev' ous
gri mace'
guar an tee'
hab' i tat
hang' ar
haz' ard ous
hearth
her' e sy
he ro' ic
hes' i tan cy
hi lar' i ous
hon' or a ble
ho ri' zon
ho tel'
hu' man
hu mane'
hy poc' ri sy
hys ter' i cal
id' i om
ig' no min y
ig no ra' mus
il lit' er ate
im pet' u ous
im' pi ous
im pla' ca ble
im pos' tor
im' po tent
im promp' tu
im' pro vise
in ap' pli ca ble
in clem' ent
in. con' gru ous
in diet' ment
in' do lent
in er' tia
in fal' li ble
in' flu ence
in quir' y
in sane'
in' ter est
in vei' gle
in' ven to ry
i ' o dine
i ' rate
ir ref' u ta ble
ir rev' o ca ble
i ' so late
i tin' er ar y

6

jo' vi al
ju di' cial
ju' ve nile
ker' o sene
ki mo' no
lam' en ta ble
lan' guage
leg' end
lei' sure
length' en
le' ver
lie' o rice
lin ge rie'
lit' er a ture
lon gev' i ty
lu' di crous
lux' u ry
ma lev' o lent
mal treat'
ma ni' a cal
mar' ma lade
mas' sa ere
mat i nee'
me dic' i nal
me di e' val
me' di o ere
mel' an chol y
me men' to
me' ni al
men' u
mer' can tile
mer i to' ri ous
me tic' u lous
min' i a ture
mi rac' u lous
mis' chie vous
mol' e cule
mon' e tary
mo rale'
mo ral' i ty
mu nic' i pal
mu se' um
naph' tha
nar ra' tor
nau' seous
nem' e sis

ni' ce ty
noc tur' nal
no' ta ble
nov' ice
nup' tial
ob lig' a to ry
ob lique'
of' ten
o' gre
om' e let
op pres' sion
or de' al
or' gy
o rig' i nal
pa cif' ic
pac' i fist
par' lia ment
pat' ent
pa' tron age
per' il ous
per' son al
per son nel'
per spi ra' tion
pi an' o
pic' ture
pit' i a ble
pleb' i scite
poign' ant
pol' i tic
pos' i tive ly
pre ced' ence
pre ced' ent (a.)
prec' e dent (n.)
pref' er a bly
pre fer' ment
prel' ate pref ty
prim' i tive
prob' a bly
prod' uce (n.)
pro duce' (v.)
prog' res (n.)
pro gress' (v.)
pro sa' ic

whim' si cal
wit' ti cism

pun' gent
qui' nine
quix ot' ic
rad' ish
ra' tion
re cu' per ate
ref er ee'
ref u gee'
re fuse' (v.)
ref' use (n.)
rep' li ca
rep' u ta ble
re' qui em
re search'
re source'
res' tau rant
ri die' u lous
ro bust'
ro mance'
route
rou tine'
ru' in ous
ruth' less
sat' ire
sched' ule
scru' pu lous
sec re tar' i al
se ere' tive
sen' a tor
ser e nade'
sham poo'
sil hou ette'
sim' i lar
sin' is ter
so' cia ble
sol' dier
squal' id
sta' di urn
sta tis' tics
sta' tus
stra te' gic
strength

xy' lo phone
yeo' ma

stren' u ous
stu pid' i ty
su perb'
su per' flu ous
su preme'
syl' la ble
sym' me try
syn' the sis

tab' er nac le
tac' i turn
tan' gi ble
tern' po rar y
ter rif' ic
tes'ta ment
the' a ter
the ol' o gy
ther mom' e ter
tor' tu ous
trag' e dy
trans par' ent
trav' erse
tre men' dous
tu mul' tu ous
tyr' an ny

ul ti ma' turn
u nan' i mous
u nique'
ur' gen cy
u' ti lize
vac' il lating
val' et
va lise'
vi car' i ous
var ri' e ty
vase
ve' he ment
ve hic' u lar
ver ba' tim
vi' a duct
vi car' i ous
vo' cab u lar y
vul' ner a ble

ze' nith
zeph' yr
zo ol' o gy

www.ingramcontent.com/pod-product-compliance
Lightning Source LLC
Chambersburg PA
CBHW080731230426
43665CB00020B/2695